WHO ARE YOU, REALLY?

WHO ARE YOU, REALLY?

Understanding Your Life's Energy

Gary Null, Ph.D.

CARROLL & GRAF PUBLISHERS, INC.

NEW YORK

First edition 1996

Carroll & Graf Publishers, Inc.
260 Fifth Avenue
New York, NY 10001

ISBN 0-7867-0326-1

Library of Congress Cataloging-in-Publication Data is
available.

Manufactured in the United States of America

CONTENTS

Contents

INTRODUCTION

Several years ago, when I least expected it, life did an about-face and I found myself needing to make a radical shift in my whole way of thinking and living. Within a few days, everything I had worked for and, more dismayingly, everything I had thought I was, were called into question. It started one evening at the end of a weekly class on nutrition I taught to a large group of students in Manhattan. My brother and I were discussing the class after everyone else had left.

"They're not getting it, Gary," my brother observed as we walked to the car. "The same people show up week after week, year after year, but nothing changes. The fat people haven't lost weight, the hyper ones haven't calmed down, the stress cases haven't relaxed. I don't think they're changing their diets at all. In fact, some of them head straight for McDonald's when your talk is over and load up on junk."

I stopped in my tracks, dumbfounded. It wasn't that all this was new to me—I'd basically known it subconsciously because I'd been seeing it—but this was the first time the whole picture had crystallized, perhaps because someone had verbalized it. Here I had dedicated my entire working life to helping people change their lives for the better, and my brother could see the terrible truth that I had failed to consciously grasp: I wasn't making a difference—not even for those who personally attended those weekly sessions. It was shocking. How could I have missed it?

I was, by then, twenty years into my career as a health educator and had become very well known. My daily afternoon show enjoyed the largest radio audiences in America in my time slot; my books on nutrition and health had been on the best-seller lists; I was much sought after as a lecturer. And all along, the idea that I had been making a difference had been the great motivating factor that had kept me working very hard. I had always operated under the assumption that I had a real mission in life—to find out the truth about health and stay healthy. I took great satisfaction from fulfilling what I considered my important, worthwhile function in society.

Now it seemed that my bright dream lay shattered at my feet under the dim light of the corner streetlamp. I didn't know which way to turn—an unfamiliar, highly disturbing feeling for me, who had always been so sure of things.

Maybe I didn't belong in the health field. Perhaps I should change careers, follow other interests. I blamed myself for not seeing the obvious. Maybe I was just too idealistic; maybe I should be satisfied to be like other nutritionists I knew who dispensed advice for years while indulging all the while in unhealthful habits such as smoking and drinking. No, I had too much integrity for that—I'd always put into practice in my own life the health rules I'd advocated. As the shock began to subside, I started to wonder about my audience. It just didn't make sense. I knew that they were intelligent. So why had they failed to take all the information they had received and apply it to making positive changes in their lives? What is there about people that keeps them from acting in their own best interests—even when they show up week after week to learn what to do? There didn't seem to be an answer.

I'd made a deep study of psychology and delved into more arcane systems for understanding personality, character, and human behavior, but I was still at a loss to explain what was going on with my students, and I felt anxious and confused. The next morning I was up at the crack of dawn, knowing that I had to get away, to think, to be alone for a few days. It didn't matter where I went; I'd just take the first plane I could to get out of New York after my midday broadcast.

Luckily, the first plane with an empty seat was headed for Arizona, and the desert has always been a special place for me. On the cross-country flight I kept puzzling about those students of natural health who ran around the corner for fast food the minute class was out. Some of them had been coming for years and could easily have passed a master's-level test in nutrition.

As the plane flew westward my mind was working full-time, flooded with memories of other incidents when people's behavior had surprised me. On one occasion I'd invited several friends to my farm in upstate New York for a weekend. Because I was busy in the city until late on Friday, I couldn't arrive ahead of the guests to take care of preparations. I didn't worry about it, though. There were just everyday things to do—putting away the groceries that had been ordered, making dinner, bedding down the animals in the barn. The caretaker always left early on Fridays, but my friends would figure it out. The group of friends I'd invited up the previous month had taken care of everything without being told. They'd started a roaring fire in the fireplace, made a great dinner, taken the goats into the barn, had the bedrooms ready to sleep in. They'd even chipped in to pay for the groceries, presenting me with a bowlful of tens and twenties when I arrived. We'd had a great time. I was looking forward to another pleasant weekend with this new group.

But when finally I arrived, at about ten o'clock, I found utter chaos. The boxes of food the organic food co-op had delivered were still on the porch; no one had put anything away. Fresh linens were available in neat piles in the laundry room, but no one had made a bed. The animals were loose in the yard, running around hungry, but the guests hadn't even made dinner for themselves, much less fed the animals. How could they just sit there when there were so many simple, obvious things that needed attention? Why hadn't someone taken charge? I had no answers to that puzzle either.

No use dwelling on the problems, I reminded myself as the plane started its descent. I knew that the time had come to stop trying to figure things out. I've always believed that if you send your questions out to the universe, your answer will come. Sometimes it comes in an unexpected form before you even formulate your questions. I needed the stillness the desert would provide. I settled back in my seat, feeling confident now that I was on the right track. Sooner or later, the answers would come.

By the time we'd landed and I'd rented a car, the sun was beginning to set and the heat of the day was subsiding. I drove out of town, toward some distant mountains, enjoying the sight of the desert changing color as the golden light gave way to dusky shadows. As night fell, I pulled to a stop, parked the car, and climbed to the top of a mesa. I was surrounded by stars, above me and on every side. It was mesmerizing.

I sat in the desert all night, in what might be called an altered state of consciousness, oblivious to everything around me. I gave no thought to tarantulas or fire ants or scorpions or rattlesnakes or any of the other dangers I'd learned about as a Boy Scout. There were millions of stars, and I felt safe there, peaceful and at one with the universe. I know that many people have had similar moments on clear nights when they experienced timelessness—they could have been at any point in history, a hundred, a thousand, or ten thousand years back, looking at the same panorama, having the same feelings. My anxiety left and I stayed there all night, enjoying a sense of unity with nature.

As the night wore on, I became more and more absorbed in the totality of the universe. I lost track of my problems and why I had come. I simply gave up my ego and listened to the silence, and as I did, I became increasingly aware of the magnificent overriding harmony of life. I felt that I was having a spiritual reawakening.

Insights began to arise within me, about the nature of human beings and our special, individual places in the universe. I understood how interrelated we are with one another, how each of us has a certain natural energy that is there for the good of the whole. Some people's energy impels them to change—to change their own circumstances and lifestyles, to change their communities, even to change the world. Some people's energy, by contrast, is channeled into adapting to what exists, and even nurturing it. Some people can naturally, and with ease, assert what they believe in, some to the point that they become leaders of others. Some people never lead; they just don't have that energy within them. But they can do the valuable work of supporting other people and enterprises, and the quality of their support can be extraordinary, of a caliber that the leaders would not be capable of.

So was one type of natural life energy better than another? Well, perhaps from my point of view when I had arrived at the farm that night and found the place in disarray, a guest or two with the dynamic, take-charge kind of energy would have been nice. But wasn't that idea really shortsighted, even selfish? After all, think of all the vital parts of society that are kept running day to day by the adaptive, supportive energies of nonleaders: farms, hospitals, stores, banks, factories. . . .

As I became immersed in that state of receptivity that allows inspiration to flow, I sensed that it was time to broaden my perspective on human behavior. People's natural life energies were too diverse to expect anyone to behave in any particular way. Perhaps the important thing was whether a person was living up to the highest potential for her or his type of energy.

At the first light of dawn, I looked around, and not too far from me was a woman, sitting very still, facing the lightest part of the sky, where the sun would soon rise. I got up and walked over to her slowly, and as I approached I realized she was an Indian, quite old, though how old I couldn't say. The deep lines etched in her face by the sun made her look ninety, although she might have been only sixty. She had the timeless quality of the stars above, still in evidence in the early light of dawn.

Thinking I might be on her land, I started to say I was sorry to have imposed, but my words seemed not to matter. She looked at me kindly and asked, "Have you found what you came for?"

"Yes, more than I could ever have hoped for," I responded. "This has been a very short journey for me, but perhaps the most significant I have ever taken."

She gestured with her hand out over the landscape where there was nothing but empty mountains and desert. "When you have nothing to lose, then everything is yours to enjoy."

I didn't know in what context she meant that, so I said, "I've made my life about acquiring knowledge and sharing that knowledge."

The woman looked at me again and said something that startled me and enabled me to see my life from a whole new perspective. "Knowledge is the most important gift you must learn to let go of."

I understood immediately. I had thought that as long as I brought people knowledge, they would use it—facts and blueprints for change that they said they wanted for their ailments—their arthritis, depression, cancer, insomnia. I really believed in the hundredth-monkey syndrome—that when enough people believe in something new and better and do something to actualize it, there's a general shift in the consciousness of the populace at large. Marilyn Ferguson had said it in *The Aquarian*

Conspiracy; Herman Kahn said it in a slightly different way: When the critical mass shifts, the paradigm shifts. Believing in these notions, I had thought I could help change things by educating people to adopt a healthier, more spiritual life.

Now, as this Indian woman's simple words sank in—"Knowledge is the most important gift you must learn to let go of"—I realized that there had been no paradigm shift, there had never been a quantitative spiritual change in the consciousness of most Americans. I had been operating on a false premise, thinking I could transmit data and change some destructive habits in the world. I knew in a second that I had to give up all my knowledge, release everything that I'd felt offered me intellectual certainty, and become a student again. The difference between the facts and the truth became very clear to me. The facts, which I had been dispensing right and left, were not the answer. I felt humble, intellectually naked. I was very thankful to the universe for all the insights into human nature it had inspired in me, and grateful to the Indian woman with her deep, intuitive wisdom. I knew I must begin again, on a new and different path. There was a lot of work ahead, many changes to be made. But I had a clear vision now of the dynamic workings of human nature, and knew what I must do to fulfill my highest potential in the great scheme of things. I couldn't just think my thoughts anymore; I had to live them. And that meant I had to change.

My first day back in the studio I made some radical changes in my program and in the way I dealt with my audience. I went on the air and really got honest. I told my audience that I couldn't help them anymore. They had been calling in because they wanted instantaneous cures for their sicknesses. But I knew that they were not using the information I was providing—some of them might have called in fifty times with questions about their arthritis, but they still had it. So I refused to give another sixty- or ninety-second answer to a question. I just couldn't dispense another fact or figure. Then I told the audience that I was turning the tables on them— instead of my getting a rating as a broadcaster, I was rating them as an audience, and they rated a zero. They were just not living up to their potential. I had been honoring them as if they were trying to be healthy, but they were working very hard at being sick.

The station manager and program director were frantically gesturing from the control room. They thought I had really gone over the edge. Of course, they decided to fire me. That would take several months, because I had a full roster of sponsors, so my program stayed on the air in the meantime. My ratings plummeted into oblivion. Before, I had received as many as twenty-five thousand phone calls during a one-hour show, which is a phenomenal number of calls. Once the telephone company circuits had actually blown out with all the busy signals they had to give. But now I was getting only three or four calls per hour, which was just as well, because I had decided that what I needed to do was put every question and answer into a context. I would provide as deep and integrated a view to my listeners as I possibly could.

If someone called in and asked about fat in a hamburger, my answer had to do with everything that was connected to the fat. I felt that I wasn't living up to my potential, living at the high end of my life energy, if I didn't put things into context for people, take the time to tell them, in depth, everything they needed to make intelligent choices for themselves. So instead of reciting the data about cholesterol counts, I told the whole story of the destruction of the rain forests to plant grass for cattle on a pasture that was only a temporary pasture because the topsoil was so thin it would not support a second growth. They heard about the decline in rainfall on the planet because of destruction of South American rain forests, about destruction of species of plants and animals, about eradication of indigenous cultures so a restaurant chain could buy cheap hamburger that is high in fat, high in sodium, high in animal protein, high in disease-producing microorganisms—none of which we need. When I was finished, they would have enough of a feel for the process to make intelligent choices for themselves about being part of the whole destructive cycle.

I had stopped living by the headlines of life, and as I changed the way I shared my knowledge with people, my life grew richer and deeper. Over the course of the following six months, while the station was looking for my replacement, the next rating book came out, and I had more than doubled my number of listeners and ended up with the largest afternoon radio audience in the United States. No one had known that this audience wanting health and wholeness was there.

DEVELOPING THE LIFE ENERGIES SYSTEM

After I made the necessary changes in my own life, I turned my attention to the amazing insights I had had about natural life energies. The theory of natural patterns of energy of human beings was, in one sense, easy to put together. So much had been given to me that starry night in the desert—a complete gestalt, a holistic view of the human race, with people naturally fitting into the total picture.

While I knew intuitively that my concepts were right on target, I realized that they needed to be expanded. Also, to convince other people of the concepts' validity, I would have to take a scientific approach to testing my hypotheses. The rule in scientific research is that you must try to disprove your own theory. If you can't, then it may have merit.

I set up some studies and enlisted the aid of several psychologists, psychiatrists, and behaviorists to see if the model worked for them. They came from different schools of psychoanalytical thought and employed different psychotherapeutic models—they were Freudians, Jungians, Gestaltists. I had received a Ph.D. in psychology myself, and though I was not in clinical practice, I had the opportunity, through my work, to meet and interview people from all walks of life.

I saw that there are different qualities in each energy that make each one uniquely valuable. I developed a range of possibilities for each energy and checked to see which kinds of people had it in them to go to certain extremes.

We tested the natural life energy theory with thousands of people, and I taught it to thousands more over the course of eight years. Those who have learned it, whether or not they are professional therapists, have found it a powerful tool for understanding themselves and others.

One thing I've found is that the natural life energy model can be really helpful in conjunction with selecting the right person for a job. For example, if you were hiring a secretary, you would want to get someone who was an energy match in the supportive role. If you were hiring a salesperson, you'd probably look for a candidate displaying aggressive energy. Also, if you were looking for a job for yourself, or starting a career, it would be particularly important that your efforts suited your energy. If you had been told all your life that you should be a lawyer, for example, but your life energy was predominantly creative, you'd do best to follow your creativity, or all your life you would be a square peg in a round hole. You'd be unhappy—and probably not a very good lawyer.

I tested the theory in my own office and found that I had someone in an important supportive position who did not have the highest level of supportive energy. I replaced that person with someone for whom reliability and dependability were second nature. She was not willing to take risks, but she was practical and efficient, and within two weeks the office started humming along. The atmosphere was harmonious, and it was easy to be there. Her life energy category was absolutely on target. I have never failed when I've set up an enterprise according to people's life energies.

In the area of personal relationships, too, looking at things from the perspective of natural life energies can be enlightening. In my own life, I reflected, I seemed to be attracted to a certain type of woman over and over again. Though the initial attraction was always compelling, this was never the kind of person I could be with for any length of time without conflict. When I applied the life energy principles to this area, they worked beautifully to help me identify that particular energy. I am still attracted to and like that particular type of woman, but I don't pursue a relationship. No matter how exciting it might be at the outset, there's no point in wasting our time and setting ourselves up for stress and anguish.

This book is the result of more than eight years of research into the natural life energies concept that began to evolve for me that night in the desert. I hope you find it valuable and easy to apply to yourself, your family, and your friends, and that you come to benefit from it as much as I have in terms of discovering a higher, more balanced use of your own energy and, through that discovery, a more satisfying life.

I extend my deep thanks and appreciation to all of the thousands of people who have contributed to our understanding, and to the powerful forces of the universe that always provide more than you'd hoped for when you take the time to quiet your mind, ask, and listen for the answer.

—Gary Null, New York
March, 1996

WHO ARE YOU, REALLY?

LIFE ENERGY AND HOW IT WORKS

Each person comes into the world with an essence, a unique constellation of attributes that make him or her different and special. We have certain capacities for physical growth and strength and for intellectual development programmed into our DNA right along with the genes that make our eyes blue and our hair brown.

One of these original attributes of the self is a unique spiritual energy that is manifested as charisma or magnetism, a dynamic quality that gives a person the ability to attract or influence other people—and maybe even the ability to attract and influence events. At one end of the spectrum of this dynamic energy are those supercharged few who have what we call "star quality," which we see played out not just on the stage but also in all of life's arenas—business, sports, religion, academia, medicine, the military.

1

At the other end of this energy spectrum are people who have no need to stand out in any way. No matter how physically strong they may be or how high their IQ, the energy of their spirit is adaptive rather than dynamic. Their joy is more low-key, their gift is their ability to adapt to circumstances and make life work no matter what.

This special life energy is separate and distinct from all other essential qualities of the self. It is impossible to measure; yet it is, I believe, the determining factor in how a person addresses life. This property of the self is what I refer to in this book as natural life energy (NLE).

When I had these insights, I was quite sure that we are all interconnected in a web of energy. No one has too much, no one has too little to fulfill his or her place in the universe. Each individual energy has its own resonance, its own note to play in this harmonious symphony called life. In a way that is truly ecological, each human being has value for and a connection to every other.

THE MAIN ENERGY TYPES

As I see it, the two main types of people in terms of natural life energy are the Dynamics and the Adaptives. The basic difference between them is that charismatic quality, a personal magnetism that enables individuals to inspire and lead others. The Dynamics are the ones who have charisma, as well as an affinity for change and often a strong sense of ego. Adaptives are not charismatic, nor are they looking to change things; their sense of ego tends to be less than that of the Dynamics. There is a third type—the Creative. Creatives have a different kind of personal rhythm, awareness, and sensitivity, which allows them—and even makes it necessary for them—to bring their creations into the world. Of course, adaptive people can be creative, dynamic people can adapt to certain things, and creative people may be dynamic or adaptive, too. What we are pinpointing when we refer to a person's natural life energy is that person's *predominant* energy type.

REFINING THE FOCUS:
THE SECONDARY QUALITIES

Within the three broad types there are further divisions: Some people are characteristically aggressive, some assertive, and some supportive.

Aggressives

The Aggressives have a driving, forceful energy and tend to lead or want to dominate others. They like to take charge of whatever they're engaged in, whether it's a business, a family, or the PTA. If you've ever been involved in an informal, unstructured meeting of several people, you've seen how the group takes on its own structure after a while, as Aggressives begin to come to the fore and assume leadership roles. There are Dynamic Aggressives and Adaptive Aggressives.

3

Assertives

Assertives put forth their own point of view with confidence. While they are willing to take an aggressive responsibility for their own actions and deeds, they have no particular need to lead others. In a group, Assertives would be the ones who are comfortable expressing their views but who are not particularly driven to take charge. There are Dynamic Assertives and Adaptive Assertives, and the Creative group consists of virtually all Creative Assertives.

Supportives

There are both Dynamic and Adaptive people who are at their best in a supportive role. Qualitatively, they are basically nurturing, happy to help, truly concerned about other people's welfare. In a group, Supportives are not the natural leaders, and they're usually not the most eloquent speakers. But they are, ultimately, the people who make things happen.

PUTTING IT ALL TOGETHER: THE SEVEN ENERGY TYPES

The three basic spiritual energies and the three basic qualities are like strands that form the warp and woof of personality. They weave together in certain patterns that produce the rich tapestry of seven NLE types. Of course,

4

there is no end to the variations that nature produces, and each person who is born is completely unique, yet everyone will fall into one of the following seven categories in terms of their predominant energy type:

Dynamic Aggressives

These people are the charismatic natural leaders of society. Think of presidents, prime ministers, generals, corporate CEOs, authority figures—they're all Dynamic Aggressives. For these self-made men and women, being goal-oriented and entrepreneurial, as well as controlling others, come naturally. You can just about feel their drive to direct things.

Dynamic Assertives

Charismatic, nonconformists, creators of social change— Dynamic Assertives, while they may be trendsetters and revolutionaries, are looking basically to control only their own lives, not others'. They know what they believe in and why, and what they don't believe in and why, because these are the types of things they think about. They are conceptually creative and process-oriented.

Dynamic Supportives

Charismatic, warmhearted, sincere, reliable, humorous, compassionate, strong yet gentle—all these words can describe Dynamic Supportives. The Dynamic Supportive energy is typified in therapists, doctors, conciliators, clergy, teachers, and communicators. Dynamic Supportives are independent, intuitive, and good at bringing people together, sometimes serving as bridges between Dynamics and Adaptives.

Adaptive Aggressives

While Adaptive Aggressives are not charismatic themselves, they are drawn to powerful people and have the resourcefulness to work with them. They are socially aware, goal-oriented, survivor types, expert at finding their niche within the power structure and using it. Successful sales and public relations people, as well as behind-the-scenes "operators," are often Adaptive Aggressives. Many actors are, too.

Adaptive Assertives

Adaptive Assertives are not charismatic, but they do have the kind of practical leadership skills that make them good foremen, supervisors, office managers, and teachers; they're solid, dependable, hard workers, and highly responsible.

Adaptive Supportives

This group comprises the great majority of the population; they are the nonglamorous supporters of the status quo, and society runs because of them. This group, which has the gift of helping others, includes workers,

secretaries, "support staff," "the troops." Sometimes se-
curity-seeking, they're also often good citizens, compassionate, charitable, even selfless.

Creative Assertives

The Creatives seem to manifest only as Creative Assertives. They often display heightened sensitivity and
perceptual ability; they're absorbed in their work, reflec-
tive, self-sufficient, sometimes volatile, visionary; they
question life and themselves. They're designers, artists,
novelists, dancers, musicians.

HIGH SIDE, LOW SIDE

The qualities I've just listed for each type of energy are
generally positive ones, and in describing people this
way I've been purposely upbeat. In truth, each NLE has
a high side and a low side, an up side and a down side.
When we are living in harmony with our NLE, we feel
comfortable within ourselves and able to live a balanced, healthy life on the high side of our energy. We
are fulfilled and able to do our best to make our special
contribution to our world, whether we are Dynamics,
Adaptives, or Creatives. We don't have to be champions
in a competition; we just need to be the best of who we
are to fulfill our life purpose.

In actuality, though, very few people are truly living
up to the potential of their energy. Perhaps this is an
unrealistic expectation; to do so you would have to be

like an athlete playing on top of his or her game every day. Yes, there is always a champion like Arnold Palmer who comes close to shooting four under par every time he goes out to play golf. Arnie plays on the high side of his golf game virtually all the time. But for every Arnold Palmer, there are millions of golfers on the course with less natural talent, interest, and determination.

On the negative end of the living-up-to-one's-potential spectrum, when we are not in touch with our innate energy at all, we may waste a great deal of time and energy trying to be what we are not. We become fragmented, unbalanced, and diseased in the process. Then we are living on the low end of our NLE, and we are unhappy and frustrated, or perhaps even dangerous to ourselves and others.

I believe that if everyone on the planet was living on the high side of his or her energy, the world would be a peaceful, joyous place. But when you look at the reality of our world today, with all its strife, pollution, crime, and political unrest, and with millions of people living dysfunctional, self-destructive lives, you can see that society is far from the harmonious whole that nature intended. A staggering number of people are living on the low side of their energies, and there doesn't seem to be a remedy in sight. Why are we so far from our natural spiritual birthright? What happens that creates misery where there should be happiness, war instead of peace?

CONDITIONING

What happens is that our conditioning often stunts or distorts our true nature. From the minute we are born, our essential being is shaped by the circumstances of our lives, and our natural life energy is influenced by these conditions. We learn from and are influenced by our families, our physical surroundings, our culture, and many other factors. We must fit in and meet the expectations of others. As we become acculturated, many layers of conditioning are superimposed over our natural selves. Much of it is useful and appropriate—we need to know how to behave in the world; we have to learn those kindergarten-level lessons about manners and traffic and consideration for others.

The problem comes when your conditioning diverts the development of your potential in a major way. Your true energy may be so blocked that you can't feel it, and as a result you may lose touch with the real you.

By the time we reach adulthood, we are an amalgam of our natural life energy, circumstances, and conditioning. If we have had positive conditioning, appropriate to our particular energy, then chances are we are ready to live a satisfying, fulfilling life. But if, instead of having had our special gifts nurtured, we have been bent to fit into a framework that is foreign to our nature, we may grin and bear it and settle for a forced kind of existence, not even acknowledging our unhappiness. We may end up spending a great deal of time and money going to groups, reading self-help books, or going to counselors and therapists to learn what makes us tick, or to find out why we're not satisfied or happy with our lives.

Here's an example of the negative effects of conditioning. A young boy is conditioned to be competitive, aggressive, ambitious, and highly driven, as boys often are; it's all intended to help him be successful, to win at any cost. So that's what he does. He fights for power and control, working hard to win recognition and enhance his self-esteem through every possible avenue. He pushes himself to get degrees, make money, achieve social standing. It looks good from the outside. But on the inside, he's living in an arid emotional desert because his real self wanted to be an artist—someone who had a cooperative rather than a competitive approach to life. He doesn't like to make other people lose so he can win; it just doesn't resonate with his spirit. But, because of his relentless conditioning, he goes ahead and gives his all to the "proper" life his family and culture have ordained for him. In doing so, he denies any connection to his natural life energy. In short, he's made an outward success of a journey down the wrong road. Only in the innermost reaches of his heart, a place where he rarely feels comfortable, does he know that the trappings of success cannot compensate for the loss of his true self.

If this individual had become an alcoholic or drug addict, or had failed at every business he'd started, it would take some doing to get through his dysfunction, but he might. Perhaps he'd go back to school as an adult, or go to support groups, to give himself a new beginning. Many people take those steps as they recover from addictions and other dysfunctional behavior. But it's a curious paradox that if this person makes a success of his career and never has glaring disasters in life, he earns so much approval from others that it becomes very hard for him to consider that he's been riding down the road through the wrong forest. In fact, he'll find it almost impossible to separate from his artificial self, renew his acquaintance with his real self, and start over. In those "wee, small hours of the morning," when his mind is quiet, the yearning will be there, but he may not even know what he longs for.

Well-meaning parents and society teach children what they think they need to know for survival: how to adapt, how to earn a steady wage, how to become integrated into society. If there's some other urge inside a child, an energy that wants to manifest itself, it can be submerged very easily at an early age by adults who think they're doing the child a favor by teaching her or him that doing well and fitting in are the most important tasks in life.

In some families, parents don't agree with each other about what conditioning to give the child, and they work at cross-purposes. The mother may be influencing the youngster to be a Creative Assertive, the father may be instilling the values of a Dynamic Aggressive, and the church may be trying to force the child into being an Adaptive Supportive. The child's natural life energy might ultimately be something different from all of these. The result can be a person who will try to manifest all of these energies, superimposed over one another, and will have trouble being himself. The person will always be confused, rarely happy.

This is not to say that each baby born is of a particular life energy type, and that it is up to the parent to figure out, as soon as possible, what type that is and then bring the child up accordingly. Being predominantly one type is something that will come much later. Young children are more amorphous than that; even though each individual has an underlying energy, as developing creatures children experiment with different energies and grow from living awhile with each (and note—in the case of very young children, "awhile" can mean a few minutes!) It's sort of like trying on different pairs of shoes—the child sees which ones fit, which ones feel even better, and which, ultimately, are the most comfortable to walk in, and give her the most joy. And just as children are periodically in need of new shoes, they periodically have to live with new energies. They try them all on for size. That's how they learn who they are.

So a parent's job is not to find a slot and then place the child into it, but rather to encourage whatever potential the child is developing at the moment. If at a particular time you as a parent find that your child's life energy seems to coincide with your own, that's fine: Your child will learn easily by example, because you are his or her best teacher. The challenge comes when your child's tendencies and your own are disparate. Then you have to let go of preconceived notions and your fear of a nature that may seem foreign to yours. People joke about not understanding their kids, but it happens all the time, and it's normal. The key is supporting your children as they metamorphose through their lives *without* your understanding them fully. You simply have to respect them.

The idea of respecting the child is fairly new in many segments of society, but now some enlightened parents and teachers are taking time to listen to children to find out what they feel ready to do. When they really know the child's inner landscape, they have a better chance of providing appropriate activities and exposing the child to things of interest. The father who wants his musically inclined son to be a quarterback, for example, might take him to concerts instead of football games, at least some of the time, to further his musical interests.

INAPPROPRIATE CONDITIONING: THE PRICE WE PAY

Conditioning can subvert our natural energy in many ways that lead to disharmony and disease. If a Dynamic Assertive woman has been taught at every turn to be subservient to the men in her life—from her father to her husband to authority in general—she will have to deny her dominant energy and learn not to let her charisma show. She may pay a very high price for that—cancer, heart disease, ulcers. Ultimately, one cannot live happily with such conflict, yet people try. They end up with psychic pain that manifests as disease.

The ideal, of course, is when a person's conditioning is attuned to her underlying nature. Generally, when I see conflict in a person, this hasn't been the case. And there are so many ways in which inappropriate conditioning occurs. The examples already given—of a boy pushed to be a Dynamic Aggressive when he was really, by nature, a Creative, and of a Dynamic Assertive girl conditioned to be an Adaptive Supportive, illustrate very common situations, but they are by no means the only ones. There are myriad variations on thoughtless conditioning, but what they all have in common is that they result in psychic pain on some level, and in waste.

13

That waste can be enormous. Some people go through their entire lives never really experiencing even the feeling of who they really are, because the moment they start to get to that feeling, they deny it. That's what they were taught to do.

I've seen it all. I've seen so many Dynamics who had to live as Adaptives. Why? Because they were conditioned to fear being their true selves. This is how it happened:

As youths, they would periodically get new ideas and attempt to act on them.

"Stay in your place," their parents said.

"I feel—"

"Don't."

"But I think—"

"Don't."

After a while, they didn't. The only problem is, they are now trapped, and on some level, they know it. Perhaps they sense that that's why their adult lives are beset by frustration and anger.

I've also seen Adaptives try to live as Dynamics, because they were conditioned to be dynamic. It didn't work, though. They were just pushy.

Sometimes a child does grow up to follow the path dictated by his or her own natural life energy, and the parents can't understand it. They view their grown child as a failure, and the irony is that the child is living a happy life, one that's right in sync with his or her essential self.

Think of two Creative Assertive types who are highly involved in the arts and who have always just assumed that their son would follow in their footsteps and become a writer or a poet or a painter or a musician. Despite years of the best schooling and special lessons, though, nothing "takes," and the son grows up and goes on to a career in an area with less glamor than those the parents have been involved in. Nor does the son have any desire to move in the same circles his parents have enjoyed. He works as a manager in a hardware store, and thus seems to have rejected everything his parents have lived by. They view him as a disappointment. It's not a monetary thing particularly, but a cultural one. Their son seems to have turned his back on their whole world.

The problem here? There is none, except in the parents' minds. Maybe the son is simply not a Creative Assertive. Maybe he's an Adaptive Assertive. Maybe if his parents had thought in terms of natural life energies, and the possibilities of people within families having different ones, their conditioning of their son would have been less one-sided. They would have been more open to life's possibilities—from their son's perspective. They would have encouraged him to enroll in business courses instead of art school when he'd shown a leaning in that direction. With a broader, life-energy-based view, they would have had no trouble seeing their child not as a failure, but as a success, because they would have seen immediately that he's happy doing what he's doing. They would have understood that in his quiet mind, he is at peace when he thinks about his life. There is no dissonance between how he is living and what he is all about.

LISTENING TO THE QUIET MIND

Your natural life energy is the mode of living you acknowledge as your own when you give yourself a quiet mind. It's the mode you're operating in when you're in your happiest, most comfortable, and most relaxed state. It is *not* the mode you're operating in—no matter how "successfully"—under pressure, be it financial or status pressure, or the pressure of conditioning.

Here's a way to visualize it. Let's say you were in a roomful of randomly selected people and you were all given art lessons. Everyone in the room would end up painting something. For some of the people in the room, the act of creating a painting would be natural. If you were part of this group, that natural feeling would show in your work, and you would have experienced a comfortable flow while working. But for others in the room, painting would be a very uncomfortable process. If you were part of this group, you wouldn't be happy with what you did, and you wouldn't have felt particularly happy doing it.

But what if you had been conditioned to always be a creative person? You could fake it; you could force it; technically, you could do it; and if you had the right connections and knew how to "talk the talk," you might even be able to base your whole life around painting. But your life wouldn't be real. And if you went on to live as a Creative Assertive when in fact your energy was a different one, you would feel terrible when you gave yourself a quiet mind.

16

People can sometimes live lives dramatically split between their true life energies and those they were conditioned to display. There was a very well known man who, at work, was a champion of industry and a major American force both in economics and in politics. But in his personal life—I was in his home many times—his wife was an absolute Dynamic Aggressive and he was an Adaptive Supportive. That's how extreme the differences can be. I talked with him on a personal level, asking him, "Where do you feel happiest?" Because, again, that's the key: Where do you feel most satisfied, comfortable, and happy?

He said, "At home."

I said, "Even, you know, with the family—"

He said, "I love it. I feel so relaxed and at ease. I feel it's like me."

"So how do you feel being this great icon of industry?"

He said he feels very uncomfortable. He said, "I have to force myself. I know I've got enemies and people think I'm this crude and harsh bastard. But look, I was told that if you want to get on in business, this is what you have to do."

His parents had both been Dynamics, and they had pushed him and pushed him and pushed him. And so he grew up believing that that's how you should be, that's how you got ahead. His conditioning was so pervasive that he accepted it. But that wasn't his real nature.

I also know a few very lucky people whose parents and schooling encouraged them to grow in the direction of their own naturally developing energies. These people tend to be more balanced and happier than those whose lives are split between an inborn and a conditioned mode of living, or those whose natural life energies have been suppressed completely.

YOU'RE NOT A PRISONER OF CONDITIONING

While conditioning is a powerful factor, it's not an insurmountable one. People can overcome it, and some people's natural life energy is so strong that they just *have* to transcend it. We probably can all think of the kid who we always knew was going to turn out a particular way because the energy was there. The conditioning didn't matter; that's how strong the energy was.

Also, it's sometimes possible to change course after living a certain way for a long period. I saw that a few years ago, after my high school reunion.

At the reunion, I was disappointed to find that one of my best friends through high school and college was not there, and that no one had heard anything as to his recent whereabouts. We knew he'd had problems—he'd been an alcoholic, he'd been on drugs, he'd had businesses that had come and gone. We were all concerned about him.

I remembered Bob as a fun guy but very aggressive; he was definitely an Adaptive Aggressive to the max— often living at the low end of that energy. I mean, I can remember in high school that, even in an intramural game, if he didn't win he'd get really angry and throw the basketball at someone. He was an exaggerator; he liked to be the center of attention; he bragged. It wasn't

that he'd had a bad upbringing; he'd had a good upbringing with loving parents, but they had tried to condition him to be an Adaptive Supportive in that they
expected him to grow into the kind of person who lives
quietly and works in a factory without calling attention
to himself—and that could never be Bob. So he seemed
to me to be acting out in his sometimes obnoxious way
as a kind of reaction to these expectations.

Anyway, his not being heard from by any of his former classmates was disturbing, so we searched for him,
calling all over the United States. But nobody knew
where he was. And I mean nobody—his biological father didn't know, his stepfather didn't know, his step-
mother didn't know—*no one* had seen him in four years.
I tried tracking him down in Los Angeles but couldn't
find him. And then, some time later, I called my older
brother, Howard, just to see how he and his family were
at Thanksgiving time. And I happened to say, "Just as a
point of curiosity, whatever happened to Bob? Remember Bob?"

And to my surprise, my brother said, "Sure I do; I just
saw him."

"You just saw Bob?—Where?"

"He dropped in here," Howard said.

"You're kidding!"

But he wasn't kidding. It turned out that Bob was
trying to keep a low profile at the moment. My brother
explained the he hadn't seen Bob in ages either—in
about a decade, in fact—but that recently there had been
a knock at the door. Howard had gone to open it, and
there was Bob, just standing there.

"He was dressed in old clothes," Howard reported.
"He kind of looked like he'd been wearing these same

clothes for a long period of time, and he said he'd lost everything. But then Bob said that he had given up on drugs, and on alcohol, too. He told me that he was in the process of changing his entire life radically, and that he didn't want the whole world to know about it just yet."

Howard went on to tell me that Bob was going back to school, studying soil science and landscaping. He was simply starting over, because he realized that where he had started the first time was on the wrong track.

As Howard explained more about our old friend's troubles, and about his new plans, I marveled at the human potential for self-understanding and transformation. Sometimes the realization of this potential can be quite dramatic, as it was in Bob's case. It seemed that Bob had been living for years through an artificially constructed self, a winning-is-everything self. When Bob began to experience the inevitable losses that are part of every personal life and career, he couldn't handle them; he took them as direct blows to his self-esteem, and so accelerated his downhill course of alcohol and drug abuse. But now, after twenty years of going down the wrong track, he was giving it all up to start over again as an autonomous person. That takes courage. But Howard assured me that Bob was at peace with himself. He was excited by the idea of starting all over again—going back to school as if he were just out of high school.

The latest news is that Bob is now the kind of person you can sit and have a nice conversation with, without feeling anxious because he's hyper, or trying to sell you something, or manipulate you, or dominate the conversation. Today Bob is an agronomist. Well, actually, he does landscaping and gardening, but he likes to describe himself as an agronomist because he is, after all, an

Adaptive Aggressive. But the point is this: He is no longer living on the low side of his energy. He's in the middle of the range of his life energy, and could even reach the high end if he added a spiritual element to his life. Bob has smoothed out the rough edges, become less aggressive and more constructive. He's come to terms with who he is, letting go of problems created by his conditioning. He does landscape work for the rich and famous, getting gratification from his connections with celebrities, and generally living a satisfying life. There's no more conflict within him.

So no, this is not a tale about someone conditioned to be an Adaptive Supportive waking up one morning and realizing that he's really a Dynamic Aggressive and going on to become president of the United States. Real-life personal growth is not usually that dramatic. But the picture is still a positive one because here we have someone who was able to fine-tune where he was in the natural life energy picture, jettisoning the low side of his Adaptive Aggressive nature, and improving his life in the process. And ultimately, improving one's life is the goal of self-understanding.

DYNAMIC AGGRESSIVES: THE ULTIMATE GO-GETTERS

There's a bit of folk wisdom to the effect that any child can grow up to become president of the United States. That may or may not be true, but it sure helps to be a Dynamic Aggressive!

Dynamic Aggressives are society's leaders and policy-makers. They are competitive, action-oriented individuals with the ability to motivate and lead others. They actively seek to control people and even influence the course of history. Social change would not be possible without the leadership of these powerful and effective people, who take every opportunity to actualize their visions. They rise to the top of their professions, and can be found in the upper echelons of government, industry, and the church. They're the ones who lead us as presidents, prime ministers, CEOs, heads of religions, and self-employed businesspeople and entrepreneurs. On the seamier side, they're the ones who take advantage of us as con artists, religious charlatans, and dictators. In short, Dynamic Aggressives are the people who, when put in an environment, will organize that environment, and sometimes exploit it.

These leadership "naturals" tend to be outgoing, intelligent, single-minded, self-reliant, and politically aware. They can also be self-centered and egotistical, and they sometimes hate to lose so much that they focus on winning at all costs. Thus they can be insensitive, manipulative, stubborn, and arrogant. They are driven people who may be too heavily focused on amassing power and money.

The day-to-day lifestyle of Dynamic Aggressives is not like that of most of us. Of course, they tend to be richer than most of us, and to live in more opulent surroundings, but a more essential difference is that relaxation is never a goal for them. You're not going to find these people watching television—unless they are on it. They're generally not into novels or drama, because their drama is their own lives. They do not seek out peace and quiet; they don't like it. What they like is action—specifically, action that they're generating. And you'll often find them surrounded by an entourage of people who help them do so.

Gathering such an entourage is not difficult for Dynamic Aggressives, who are so charismatic that they attract other people without even trying. Their ability to command the loyalty of others seems almost effortless. People believe in Dynamic Aggressives, they trust them, and they are willing to work with them. This loyalty can be attributed, in no small part, to the visionary drive of this group. They see the big picture in life and generally have designs on changing it. So on their up side, these people can make the world a better place.

Dynamic Aggressives have gestalt minds—everything is instantly seen. If you show them a lake, they visualize what could be done to develop it. If you show them a hill, they see beyond the obvious cluster of trees and develop an immediate picture of its possibilities. Once they see the whole picture, they work backwards to figure out how to implement their vision. Then they rally others to help realize the vision, since they are poor at detail work themselves.

In fact, many Dynamic Aggressives are not highly educated people for this same reason. The educational system, especially at the doctorate level, requires too much detail work and follow-through for the Dynamic Aggressive. These are impatient people who want things to happen now, and they don't want to get bogged down in the process. It's not that they're afraid to dig in and work, but rather that skipping the details and delegating them to others is a way they can keep their own momentum going full throttle. And Dynamic Aggressives are excellent at motivating others and forming teams to get a job done.

However, they tend to be more competitive than cooperative, and their first loyalty is to themselves. They have strong egos; they want to win, and they want to be right. They don't go around any obstacles they encounter; they go over them. Still, on their up side Dynamic Aggressives can be compassionate people with little pretense to them. When their natural charm and dynamic energies are put to use, they can be very beneficial to the world. After all, they're the ones who take risks that no one else would dream of taking, and do things that no one else would dream of doing. They're opportunity-grabbers. And that's the kind of activism that real progress is made of.

A Dynamic Aggressive on the down side is another matter entirely. At this end of the spectrum, Dynamic Aggressives are extremely demanding and can push others to the edge with their criticism. Emotionally, they may be cold and unengaging because they are shut down themselves. Surprisingly, this lack of emotion can create a sense of mystery that attracts others. There's a certain appeal about a person who is not an open book—although some of these people seem to have reached the extreme of having their pages permanently glued together! They continue to attract, though. Many people who are not otherwise passive will simply accept a Dynamic Aggressive's hostility and negative energy because they are drawn to their powerful qualities.

Power is everything to a Dynamic Aggressive, and vulnerability is something to be swept under the rug. So this group generally doesn't talk about pain; they suffer quietly. As for drug abuse, this is not an issue for Dynamic Aggressives, because drugs would make them lose their all-important control, or at the very least, sidetrack them. Also, it's rare that one of these go-getters is slowed down by illness. Nor are they slowed down by poverty. They thrive in it—briefly—until they work themselves out of it and get as far away from it as possible, ultimately establishing themselves as the complete antithesis of poverty in some grand setting or other.

The Dynamic Aggressive's dominant role among people is mirrored in other areas of the animal kingdom. Even in a group of animals that dominates others, you will find one that rules the other dominant types. One lion will lead other lions, for example. Dynamic Aggressive people operate in much the same way. You will never see two Dynamic Aggressives with equal control; one is always the dominant member of the group. Other people seem to sense who is the strongest member of a group and acknowledge that power.

What would happen if we had no Dynamic Aggressives? We'd have no societal growth. This energy leads the quest for change in every part of our social fabric. Someone who's not infused with this particular energy will not go out and start a reform movement or a corporation—at least not successfully. It takes a certain measure of stamina, courage, and self-confidence—egotism, actually—to face adversity and get to the top.

Once at the top, the Dynamic Aggressive faces enormous challenges—in the case of political leaders, for instance, the challenge of creating a greater vision of society and then actualizing it. To do these things, the leader has to inspire confidence and trust, and, given some charisma and good handlers, this part of his task is highly doable. In fact, we as a nation seem quite ready to blindly follow our leaders, banking our trust in them the way we leave money in the bank—unchecked for long periods.

The trouble comes when there is competing leadership that prompts us to face the fact that our trust has been betrayed. Examples abound: We were told by the presidential candidate that taxes would be cut, but now that he's president, they've been increased. We were told that he disliked PAC groups, but now we find that he's accepted vast sums of money from them. These examples of misplaced trust, part of Bill Clinton's political problems now, are typical of how the Dynamic Aggressive politician can get himself into hot water.

No Dynamic Aggressive simply wakes up one day and finds himself or herself in a position of leadership. Our societal heads go through enormous battles to get there. The average person would find these battles too overwhelming and the game too tough to play, but the true Dynamic Aggressive does not. They become combatants to reach their positions; being a warrior is a rite of passage required of all leaders in our society.

Therefore, society must be careful of Dynamic Aggressives when they are on their down side, because these are practiced warriors who are seeking to control everything in their environment, including other people. A predatory Dynamic Aggressive will seek out relationships and environments that can be controlled to his or her advantage, no matter what that control means for others. And the Dynamic Aggressive is like the great white shark—without natural predators. So they can be extremely dangerous.

Consider the nature of corporate takeover artists. These people didn't learn to be takeover giants in school. If that were the case, then the millions of people who got more degrees than they did would have done the same. They did not, for the simple reason that they don't have the type of charismatic energy possessed by Dynamic Aggressives—charisma that allows them to attract other people and work through their energy. Dynamic Aggressives are masters at using the power given to them by others. Machiavelli wrote the book, and other Dynamic Aggressives follow it.

On their down side, Dynamic Aggressives have no loyalty at all. They assume that loyalty is due to them,

28

not the other way around. In fact, they can be quite sensitive about the issue of loyalty. They'll pay for it if they must, by giving power and prestige to their loyal supporters. Unfortunately, they fail to recognize that loyalty can never really be bought, that it's not a commodity to be given and taken away.

Why, then, are we continually drawn to Dynamic Aggressives? The reason is that we get something important from them: a deeper understanding of the meaning of life. Throughout history, Dynamic Aggressives have interpreted the larger meanings of life for other people. So rightly or wrongly, we choose to follow them and live by their teachings. The best example of this phenomenon are the many priests and spiritual leaders who are Dynamic Aggressives.

This energy group has some very skilled orators, although their charismatic communications skills are generally one-way; that is, they're not great listeners. But because they speak so well, Dynamic Aggressives can develop a large following. The question is: What do they do with their magnetic and visionary qualities? At one extreme, they may treat others with benevolence and focus on making the world a better place. At the other end of the spectrum, they may be utterly ruthless and deceptive people, such as Adolf Hitler, Julius Caesar, and Genghis Khan. Either way, the rest of us will change our way of thinking—even our whole way of looking at the world—at their say-so. They're the paradigm makers and breakers.

In this regard, a fascinating example of a Dynamic Aggressive was Jesus Christ. Christ was not merely an Assertive who sought power and control over his own life; rather, he sought to influence the lives of others. So he was a true Dynamic Aggressive, albeit not today's money- and status-hungry type. But he, too, had an up side and a down side. In the latter, he experienced pain, denial, guilt, and fear. He did learn from those periods and returned to the high side of his energy. Likewise, Martin Luther King, Jr., was a Dynamic Aggressive who actively sought to change our society. He had strength and vision, and he developed the allegiance of others and put it to his use. His down side was characterized by the marital affairs that others used against him.

There are fewer examples of female Dynamic Aggressives, probably because society suppresses the mechanisms of this energy type in women. Those who do surface, much like their male counterparts, may be destructive in manifesting their energy. They can be self-interested and controlling—witness Margaret Thatcher—but their charisma is not forced. They come by it naturally and express it at a very high level. The average woman could never evolve into a Margaret Thatcher. If you took the most educated woman and made her prime minister of England, she would not have the same effect. The missing element? Margaret Thatcher's natural Dynamic Aggressive energy.

Female Dynamic Aggressives must overcome considerable odds to express their energy. Throughout history, these women have not been given the same opportunities as men to demonstrate their unique characteristics, with the rare exception of a few heroine warriors. For the most part, women have had to express their Dynamic Aggressive qualities through socially acceptable channels, such as writing. And even as writers, women were not at all acceptable until the mid-1800s.

By withholding the opportunity to excel from many

women, society may be especially repressive of female Dynamic Aggressives. The ones we do see may seem at times particularly pushy and obnoxious. But they probably have to be, to get anywhere. Remember, in the top levels of society these women are competing in a male milieu, so they may have to take on typically male characteristics and ways of doing things to get anyone's attention. And there's a double standard about what's considered pushy and obnoxious in a man versus in a woman.

By the way, if you're having trouble conjuring up a mental image of any Dynamic Aggressive, male or female, whom you know personally, you may not know one. In fact, there's a good chance that you've never even met one, because this is the smallest energy group; only about 0.5 percent of the population is Dynamic Aggressive. Actually, the majority of the population does not belong to any Dynamic energy group at all, but is, rather, Adaptive. Yet it's part of the go-getter mentality—or perhaps mythology—of this country that we're all "supposed to" be like the Dynamics. But this is just not human nature for the majority of us.

At any rate, the rarity of this particular energy subcategory is a good thing; if we had too many Dynamic Aggressives milling around in society, the conflict level would be incredible. These highly territorial people— and those they got to follow them—would be destroying each other right and left, and the environment would be more of a shambles than it already is. Plus nobody would be willing to deliver the mail, to drive a cab, or to farm the land—what was left of it! So it's a good thing this group is not more prevalent.

Of course, if you *have* met a Dynamic Aggressive, you

no doubt remember the occasion. When one of these people enters a room, everyone else in it sits up and takes notice; there's just no way you can miss one. It's not that Dynamic Aggressives necessarily have hyperactive mannerisms or a loud, attention-seeking demeanor. On the contrary, they are often quiet, calm, methodical people. But they radiate an unmistakable energy that can only be described as intimidating.

How do Dynamic Aggressives get to be the way they are? Neither conditioning nor heredity are particularly relevant; it's a matter of a special energy that lies within. So it doesn't matter how they were taught, or what school they went to, or what their parents were like, or what foods they ate. Instead of the old saw "Blood will tell," we should think of the phrase "Life energy will tell," because this is certainly true in the case of society's leaders.

UP SIDE/DOWN SIDE: A WHOLE WORLD OF DIFFERENCE

Because the Dynamic Aggressive is the most powerful of energy types, the difference between his up side and his down side can be tremendous. Indeed, the chasm between the two sides of this energy can have serious implications for the rest of society. On their up side, Dynamic Aggressives can be great spiritual leaders who galvanize an organization or an entire nation. On their down side, they have the potential to become a Hitler or a Stalin. And here's a scary thought: You and I might not want to be in a war, but if the two people who head our governments are Dynamic Aggressives on their down side, we may end up shooting and killing each other for reasons that are totally absurd. It's happened—too many times.

Think about politics, and the Dynamic Aggressives who run government. I find it interesting that these people generally tell others that they subscribe to traditional values. In many cases, though, this statement is merely a tool that allows them to attract the loyalty of Adaptive Supportives and maintain control. In reality, the Dynamic Aggressive's values are all his or her own. If left unchecked, the Dynamic Aggressive will exercise a compulsive, almost addictive need to influence others. As leaders in politics, industry, and religion, they will use whatever dogma exists in society to control others. Witness the ability of the church to thrive on conformity, dogma, and ritual.

Dynamic Aggressives on the down side are prone to gross depression, acute anxiety, and a hostile attitude toward anyone who stands in their way. If they fail at an endeavor due to these obstacles, they will start again, but remain extremely vengeful. Dynamic Aggressives never forget the people who played a part in their failure.

One of the most harmful forces known to man is a Dynamic Aggressive motivated by hate. You end up with someone such as Saddam Hussein, whose charisma and negative energy, when combined with his ability to make policy, led to the death of many people.

On a higher side of their energy, Dynamic Aggressives will convert their negativity into pragmatism. They have a realistic view of life that allows them to move beyond the cynicism that mires other energy types in negative inactivity. Many people can never see the good in life because they are consumed by what is bleak, disturbing, and wrong in the world. The Dynamic Aggressive can overcome this cynicism, take an optimistic view of the world's chances for improvement, and work to that end. Look at Jimmy Carter and his work to house the homeless and mediate conflicts. Dynamic Aggressives make excellent mediators, by the way, if only because they're so practiced at the art of the deal.

On the high end, Dynamic Aggressives who are connected with their spiritual sides are conscientious and balanced individuals, and their aggressiveness becomes a positive, constructive quality. A Dynamic Aggressive operating at this level can improve the environment, uplift people spiritually, make a company operate in a more responsible way, and change the world for the better.

A Dynamic Aggressive may evolve from the low side of his or her energy to the higher-end qualities. Early in life, many of this country's robber barons were ruthless in their treatment of the environment and other human beings. Through a metamorphosis of some sort, they later came to understand that they were abusing their power. These people, such as Carnegie and Rockefeller, then tried to make amends through philanthropic works and foundations.

Unfortunately, though, history shows us that, in general, Dynamic Aggressives do not operate from their higher energies. Since civilization's beginnings we have had only 230 years of world peace, in part because those with Dynamic Aggressive energy seek unconditional power and control. They lose their connection with the world around them and begin to believe that all others are there to serve their needs. Thus politicians are bought, judges are bribed, and anyone in their path becomes a manipulatable object, to the point of becoming cannon fodder.

THE WORK OF DYNAMIC AGGRESSIVES: MOVING AND SHAKING

One way of describing the Dynamic Aggressive is simply to say that this is the type of person who goes after it—and gets it. You (unless you are a Dynamic Aggressive) and I would never go after it to begin with; it's not part of our energy. Even if we were forced to go after it, we wouldn't feel good about it, and we wouldn't be going for it with the same passion that Dynamic Aggressives do. But they're the ones with the predatory passion, and in a broad sense, getting what they want is their life's work. In doing so, they move and shake the world.

In terms of occupation, Dynamic Aggressives are only satisfied with policy-making positions that allow them to manifest their energies, whether in politics, business, banking, or religion. In any of these fields, they tend to rise to the top and become leaders. If a particular position does not have the promise of power and control, the person with this energy moves on to something else. Staying in one place for a long time is not something they're good at; in fact, it's not unusual for Dynamic Aggressives to make a dozen career changes along the way. When they finally solidify their position of power—say, in the real-estate field—others can see that their background is all over the place, in areas that have nothing to do with real estate.

In many cases, Dynamic Aggressives start off as careerists in their chosen field and then give that field up totally to pursue other interests. For example, a Dynamic Aggressive who becomes a doctor may tire of the politics involved in the profession and decide to do something else instead. They're not afraid of loss, and they rarely worry about their ability to make money, a task that is not usually a problem for them.

Generally, the Dynamic Aggressive's ultimate professional goal is to work for himself or herself. At the start of their careers, they will do a lot of job-hopping—for example, from industry to government and back to industry again—to gain the skills they need to strike out on their own. Eventually most Dynamic Aggressives will end up working for themselves. They are entrepreneurial by nature, and they dislike working for others. They rarely last in corporations unless they rise quickly to the top, because they don't want to join the club for long and follow the policies of others. They want to be the policy-makers themselves.

Still, on their up side, they *can* work in harmony with others. They have constructive ideas about what needs to be done, and they work hard to achieve those goals. If the hard-driving leadership qualities of the Dynamic Aggressive are balanced with the high-end qualities of other energy types, a lot of positive work can be accomplished. The thing to remember, though, is that the work of the Dynamic Aggressive is always to some extent self-directed, in the sense that these people are individual careerists who work on themselves as much as they work on the projects at hand.

Once they're in charge, Dynamic Aggressives tend to have Adaptive Aggressives working at the level right beneath them—witness Reagan and Oliver North, or Hitler and Goebbels, for some non-high-end examples. The Adaptive Aggressive group doesn't have the charisma of the Dynamics—which is good because there's no challenge there—but they do have the drive and know-how to implement the Dynamic Aggressives' policies. And the Dynamic Aggressive does need good implementers, because detail work is not his forte. Indeed, not taking care of details can be a real problem for these broad-stroke visionaries.

I can illustrate this from personal experience. I have a Dynamic Aggressive friend who has a beautiful house. But since he never takes care of anything, none of the doors work. It's a nine-million-dollar house, and yet you go out to get a newspaper in the morning and none of the doors works to let you back in! This happened to me when I was a houseguest, and since the bell was non-functional and my friend was asleep, I decided to jog down the road to a service station to phone him so I could get back into the house. But the electric fence didn't work, so I couldn't get off the property! What I finally did was to climb in a window, which I could do because it was broken.

I got my friend up and we decided to have brunch out on the terrace. Of course, the table was cracked. We decided to take a sauna, but the sauna board broke; we landed on the floor. The Jacuzzi had some kind of scuzz in it; I wouldn't even get in it because no one had thought about throwing in anything to kill the bacteria. The swimming pool hadn't been skimmed, and I could just visualize the phantom of the black lagoon coming up, or some rare and exotic snake that happened to have been in the neighborhood, crawled through the electric fence, and decided to go for an uninterrupted swim. I myself decided not to.

And this was just his house. Another time, we went to a castle that he owned in France—a magnificent eleven-hundred-year-old castle that he'd bought for a song and that even came with its own village. This is typical of how a Dynamic Aggressive operates; they always make great deals. The only thing was, the castle needed extensive repair. There were four walls to the place, and that was about it.

"I've got all the paint here," my friend said.

"I think we need more than a few gallons of paint," I pointed out. "I think we need a construction engineer, carpenters, and contractors. I think you need to completely rebuild the entire place, because all you really have is the walls."

It turned out that he had to spend some three and a half million dollars to get the castle ready for occupancy, but then, of course, he forgot a few little details, such as provisions for turning on the heat. No, detail work was not his strong suit!

As bosses, while Dynamic Aggressives are often aloof and even hostile, when they pepper that general tone with a little positive feedback now and then, people respond very gratefully. Dynamic Aggressives seem to sense just how much partial reinforcement to sprinkle into their interactions with underlings to achieve optimum benefit.

You will rarely find a Dynamic Aggressive having a long conversation on the telephone. Whatever it is, they want to get it said and get on with it—even in the case of a personal call. If you want to meet with them, fine, but it's like this—where, when, why, good-bye. It's nothing personal, but chatting is just not on the Dynamic Aggressive's agenda. You could say that "Time is money," but you could also say that "Time is life," and the Dynamic Aggressive's life is just too full of action for aimless talk to be part of it.

One of the most important people a Dynamic Aggressive needs is his or her spokesperson or "interpreter." Dynamic Aggressives tend to react with anger, and they rarely edit themselves. In a crisis situation, they will come in, take charge, and get the job done. But they don't want the public to see or hear the process, so they hire a buffer—a spokesperson—to handle the communications. This approach is not necessarily negative; it's simply part of what it takes to get the job done.

An interesting characteristic of Dynamic Aggressives' modus operandi is that they know how to use other people's money and influence to get what they need, while most of the rest of the world has to chance using their own. So when Dynamic Aggressives lose, they don't generally lose as much.

And when they win, they win plenty, sometimes at a huge cost not just to other people, but to the environment itself. They use the environment to their advantage, whether that means strip mining, overfishing, or digging deep wells in the ocean that cause pollution. Think about who controls environment-damaging companies. It's not the average guy, the Adaptive Supportive. It's not millions of Adaptive Supportives who have banded together. It's always a relatively small number of Dynamic Aggressives who control millions of other people, and ultimately the fate of the land.

Success and the Dynamic Aggressive

In the end, most Dynamic Aggressives define success by the amount of power, control, and money they amass. A Dynamic Aggressive at the helm of a corporation does not want the business to remain small and stable; he or she may keep extending the company until it eventually ends up in financial trouble. Perhaps the core business makes money but the subsidiaries do not, and thus the process of stripping it back down begins. The point is, these achievers par excellence are not satisfied with one company and a few products. They always want more and will overextend themselves to achieve their goals. Success for them is an ever-expanding thing.

An interesting aspect of this energy type, which is generally seen as the most successful group, is that Dynamic Aggressives actually fail more than most others would ever fail. The difference is that, when most others fail, that may be it—they won't try again—but Dynamic Aggressives consider dropping down and failing to be just one part of the larger process of getting where they're going. And Dynamic Aggressives *always* get there, even if we sometimes have to pay by learning the kind of lesson you later read about in history books.

Dynamic Aggressives like to do things on a grand scale, so once they have it made, they often acquire magnificent homes. The house becomes an extension of their power, boosting their self-esteem and satisfying their need to be recognized. You never see the chairman of the board of a big company living frugally. But despite all they own—the yachts, mansions, and expensive

40

goods—Dynamic Aggressives don't know how to relax and enjoy their possessions. Instead, they fill the house with people—their entourage—every minute of the day.

In fact, Dynamic Aggressives rarely spend time alone; they need people around them at all times. Their lives are achievement-oriented, and they get depressed if people don't know about their successes. They'll hire publicists to plaster their names on billboards and in newspapers to make sure the world knows about them. Call it insecurity-motivated, which it no doubt is to a large extent, but publicity is a vital component of success for this group.

RELATIONSHIPS

If you are in a relationship with a Dynamic Aggressive, you'd better be careful; although if you are an Adaptive Supportive, you probably don't have to worry; you're not going to be having much of a relationship with a Dynamic Aggressive, unless you want to go into slavery! Generally, the Dynamic Aggressive is going to seek out people like the Adaptive Aggressive, both at work and in relationships. These are people who share the drive of the Dynamic Aggressive, but, without the charisma, do not pose a threat.

Actually, it's difficult for Dynamic Aggressives to get into any kind of deep relationship. To them, life is the relationship. That's their first obligation, their first loyalty. Their loyalty to individuals is secondary.

Generally, Dynamic Aggressives will develop a relationship with one highly trusted person, in whom they confide. They want a relationship that makes them feel safe and protected because they thrive on loyalty—the kind that is given *to* them. So you could say that these are the type of people who, rather than falling in love, fall in need. If a Dynamic Aggressive is threatened by a relationship, he or she will abandon it in a second. But the same quality that allows them to do this can also make them exciting partners. Dynamic Aggressives are not burdened by feelings of jealousy and possessiveness because they are used to having things and then moving on. Whereas most other people don't get off the starting block, the Dynamic Aggressive has already been there and back.

In lieu of true friendships, which they rarely develop, Dynamic Aggressives associate with people who have positions of power similar to their own. They acknowledge only those people they believe to be their equals, and intentionally avoid anyone who does not serve their needs. They may be cordial to others, and they will surround themselves with Adaptive Aggressives for purely practical reasons—these people help them to function. But when it comes to developing real friendships, Dynamic Aggressives generally fall short because they will not reveal their true selves. They fear vulnerability and want to minimize the risk that others will take advantage of them.

Dynamic Aggressives always have an agenda, and this is true in the relationship arena as well as that of work. As long as the other person meets those expectations, the Dynamic Aggressive has no reason to end the relationship. But they bore easily and are rarely monogamous. They often have multiple—if shallow—relationships, and they believe that all other people are there to

42

meet their needs. It's as if they view their partners as "service" people of some sort.

Thus the men may have mistresses. And some use call girls, interestingly, not so much for sex, but as confidantes. These leaders of society, who seem to have everything, often have absolutely no one to talk to, in the sense of revealing their innermost thoughts and feelings. They can't appear vulnerable to those who are part of their circle, and this includes their wives, who are often Adaptive Aggressives who might take advantage of any revelations. Often the Dynamic Aggressive can't even talk to a psychiatrist or psychologist because the fact that they needed one might leak out and jeopardize a run for public office.

Do you have a Dynamic Aggressive neighbor? That's good, not because it brings up property values, but because if he or she has any problem with you, he'll confront you directly in a straightforward way, at the outset. He won't play any silly vengeful neighbor games, whereas some members of other, less busy energy groups sometimes seem to thrive on these.

In general, the only people Dynamic Aggressives really need to stay away from are other Dynamic Aggressives. Together, two members of this energy group would attempt to control each other, leading to high-level competition and constant conflict.

On the other hand, Dynamic Aggressives can form strong relationships with Adaptive Aggressives, who will provide them with protection, carry out much of their work, and remain loyal. An Adaptive Aggressive also can handle the volatility of Dynamic Aggressives. Whereas other energy types might take a Dynamic Aggressive's outburst personally, the Adaptive Aggressive does not.

Female Dynamic Aggressives may have some problems in their relationships with men. If the man is too passive, the Dynamic Aggressive woman may quickly become bored with him. But these extraordinary women can have a hard time finding men who are not intimidated by them or obsessed with possessing them. And they may experience a lot of clashing and competition with another charismatic energy, such as a Dynamic Assertive or Dynamic Aggressive man.

A Dynamic Aggressive man and woman, in fact, are likely to have an intense and tumultuous relationship. The union would be lacking in a couple of vital elements: a sense of calm and an ability to relax. Imagine these two on a tropical island for a week of vacation. Within days, they would select a site for a new home, open up a tennis court, and figure out how to buy the island and finance the purchase with cheap bonds!

Life with a Dynamic Assertive man can be difficult for the Dynamic Aggressive woman, too. This would be a tough relationship because both have a difficult time compromising, apologizing, and acknowledging mistakes. A better bet for the Dynamic Aggressive woman would be the Dynamic Supportive man, who would be intelligent, worldly, and trustworthy, but not highly competitive.

The Parent Trap—Dynamic-Aggressive Style

In the area of parenting, an unfortunate energy combination would be a Dynamic Aggressive father and an

Adaptive Supportive mother. The children would see again and again that their mother does not stand up to a dominating father—a pattern that will in no way benefit them.

But whatever the parental combination, it's not easy being the child of a Dynamic Aggressive; their children are apt to get caught in the trap of excessive parental expectations. Dynamic Aggressives are tough on their offspring; they tend to demand that the children be every bit as ruthless and successful as they are. There's an aggressive nature to the family dynamics. And the children may be raised in an austere fashion because the Dynamic Aggressive wants them to work for what they get—just as he or she had to do. The ultimate goal is to ensure that the children have the same material success as the parent.

Thus Dynamic Aggressives will support their children, but that support is usually conditional. The kids are acknowledged when they do what the parent expects of them, or, better yet, when they do something that makes the parent feel good about who he or she is. But the lack of unconditional love in these children's lives can lead to tragic results—they may become alcoholics, drug addicts, or even suicidal. They feel constant pressure to succeed and to fulfill their parent's expectations. If they don't, the Dynamic Aggressive will let them know that something must be wrong with them. How could they "fail" when the parent gave them so much? This cynical view of life can lead the child to the mistaken belief that all people are equally emotionally ungiving.

45

GROWTH AND TRANSFORMATION

Dynamic Aggressives have a rich, full personal life in the sense that they have a lot of peak experiences. That's because they're the ones willing to take the risks, and with risk-taking comes the opportunity for self-actualization. So if you want to point to a particular beauty of the Dynamic Aggressive life, you could say that these people are exquisitely attuned to their capabilities and use them to live life to the fullest.

While individuals in this group are astute enough to be attuned to their natural energy, they may be lacking a connection to their spiritual self. But nothing improves in life unless we pay attention to our spiritual energy. When that attention is composed of decency, ethics, and morality, our natural energy will manifest at the highest level. We might create products that benefit society or, at the very least, do not hurt others.

As Dynamic Aggressives begin to earn money and get ahead in life, they may forget the spiritual part of the equation. Indeed, the equation can become strictly intellectual. If they are smarter and faster than those around them, they can get ahead early in life by making better deals. But they may fail to consider what is good for others as they pursue their goals.

On the other hand, many Dynamic Aggressives use their power to support important causes but keep a low profile about this aspect of themselves. Some examples are Armand Hammer, the former head of Occidental Petroleum; Walter Annenberg, the founder of *TV Guide;*

and several members of the Mellon family. Without such people, many of the greatest art collections in the world would not be available for the rest of us to see.

In some cases, Dynamic Aggressives learn the lessons of giving early on and support such causes throughout their lives. In other instances, a Dynamic Aggressive may realize toward the end of his life that he has overlooked certain values. He then decides—perhaps out of remorse or a fear of death—to give something back to society by supporting a cause. But the fact remains that there are many great monuments we can enjoy today due to the direct action of Dynamic Aggressives.

So Dynamic Aggressives are capable of transforming their energy dramatically. They become less interested in wielding power and more concerned with achieving greater harmony in life. They may not go out and better the world, but they will try to understand their place within it. This can be a humbling experience that changes a Dynamic Aggressive's perspective on everything. They may finally accept that all of their money, power, and prestige do not make them immortal.

IF YOU ARE A DYNAMIC AGGRESSIVE

Although fewer than one in two hundred people is a Dynamic Aggressive, there is a chance that you are manifesting this energy. If so, there's something important that you should do: Examine the role of your childhood conditioning in your behavior today. I say this because, as a Dynamic Aggressive, you can have an enormous impact on the lives of others; therefore you must strive to be as self-aware as possible.

Start by considering the type of early conditioning your own parents received. If their parents or grandparents treated them as commodities—to be influenced and used to serve their purposes—then your parents may have passed that same conditioning on to you. If so, you may be lacking in compassion and emotional rapport as an adult, which would lead you to view other people as mere objects. Dynamic Aggressives who receive unconditional love as children still have an aggressive energy, but it is tempered by their parents' acceptance of them.

If your parents were especially strict, recognize that you may be a difficult person to get along with. No doubt you expect a herculean effort, if not perfection, from everyone around you. Because you are determined to work through a problem, you want everyone else to exhibit the same sense of commitment and discipline.

Dynamic Aggressives who did not receive unconditional love as children tend to distrust other people. If this is true of your upbringing, the unfortunate reality is that you may ultimately distrust yourself as well. Dynamic Aggressives are often fearful that they will one day be exposed as shams; this is the case for so many leaders and power brokers in our world. While they need the attention and adulation of the public, they are terrified of any real intimacy with people because of this underlying feeling of inadequacy.

In an ideal world, Dynamic Aggressives would use their charismatic energy as a catalyst—a lightning rod of sorts—to make other people more conscious of their own potential. Rather than spend all their time on their own projects, these charismatic leaders would apply their energy toward motivating others and moving them toward constructive change.

If you want to work in this constructive way, you must be aware that your energy can swing from high to low at any time. Actually, all of us must recognize that there is a duality to our energy that continually challenges us. If we ignore this challenge, we're never happy and we're never healthy. Putting our energy to good use is an active process that we must constantly reaffirm if we are to avoid the cycles that can lead to negative and destructive results.

Finally, recognize that some events in life—such as a serious illness—will not be assuaged by a long list of accomplishments. You need to develop your resiliency, and thus your ability to handle such life events, by becoming more flexible and more open to others. Learn to acknowledge your own mistakes and the accomplishments of others. Show some gratitude and loyalty to those who assist you in life. These changes will not only strengthen your relationships but also set the stage for your own transformation.

THE MIND-POWERED WORLD OF DYNAMIC ASSERTIVES

They're the ones who show us the way. Like Dynamic Aggressives, Dynamic Assertives seek to guide us, but they do so by using only their highly developed powers of the mind and of self-expression, never by force or coercion.

Dynamic Assertives are rare people in our society. They have a forceful personal magnetism and an energy of mind that distinguishes them from all other energy types. They may represent a small percentage of the population (I'd say about one in a hundred people is a Dynamic Assertive), but they transform existing systems for everyone by challenging the status quo. Without them, society would not progress.

Above all, this powerhouse of an energy group is engaged with life. They try to live it to its fullest, all the while pondering its meaning in a lifelong quest for understanding. Dynamic Assertives see the big picture in the world around them and identify areas in need of constructive change. When manifesting their energy at its highest level, Dynamic Assertives will challenge the injustices that oppress us all. They will achieve breakthroughs and set trends in their chosen field, be it business, science, education, literature, or philosophy. They are spiritual, ethical, and intellectual illuminators, human beacons lighting the way to social change.

Here's a thumbnail description of a Dynamic Assertive: *the kind of person you could have a conversation with and then write an article about it.* These are free-flow, stream-of-consciousness people. They take an idea and go with it, not recognizing boundaries or limitations. Talking with them can be a sort of awakening—if you can deal with it. Dynamic Assertives can be intimidating because they don't recognize barriers—social, sexual, economic, or any other kind of barriers. So you might begin talking with one and then say to yourself, "What am I getting into? Can I handle this?" If you can, you're in for an exciting ride.

Since limitation is not part of their gestalt, Dynamic Assertives thrive on change. They believe in the very idea of change and in the limitless possibilities it implies. Ultimately they serve as the "correctors" in society, the people who can identify wrongs and have the courage to correct them. Think of Mahatma Gandhi, Robert Kennedy, Nelson Mandela, Margaret Mead, Thoreau, Spinoza, Plato, and Socrates. These are people who held a mirror up to society and said, "Take a close look. Do you like what you see? Is what you see, what should be?" In asking these kinds of questions, Dynamic Assertives break the ground for new roads upon which everyone else will eventually travel.

Dynamic Assertives are found in every stratum of society; they don't necessarily rise to the top of businesses and organizations the way the more goal-oriented Dynamic Aggressives do. So these people are not necessarily names in the news; in fact, most aren't. Some are—Ralph Nader, Dr. Benjamin Spock, and Eleanor Roosevelt are Dynamic Assertives we've all heard of— but there are also people in our midst who hold regular jobs and are not in the least famous but who definitely manifest this life energy. Have you known any? If so, you'll probably be able to count them on one hand. You'll surely have vivid memories of them because they tend to be, in the *Reader's Digest* phrase, our "most unforgettable characters."

Many Dynamic Assertives distrust authority, which they believe to operate from a self-interested agenda. They will sacrifice all to challenge such authority and facilitate change. As a result, Dynamic Assertives are a threat to established power and often end up being booted from institutions, discredited in their fields, locked away in prison, or even killed. They're martyr material. Consider Nelson Mandela, who spent nearly three decades in prison in South Africa for opposing the policies of a ruling class that oppressed millions. He was a danger to these rulers, so they attempted to silence him by sweeping him out of the way.

In fact, Dynamic Assertives generally are the first to be destroyed in a revolution of any sort. The authorities want to stop these nonconformists before they can cause a critical shift in perspective among other energy types, particularly Adaptive Supportives, who have the strength of numbers but rarely challenge authority on their own initiative. When enough Dynamic energies get together, they can focus the consciousness of many into a mass call for change; consider the Declaration of Independence and the genesis of the American Revolution. More recently in our history, consider how a small core of Dynamic Assertives sparked the movement to end the Vietnam War. And on the socio-ecological front, you may remember the time when concern for the environment was not part of any political or educational agenda. It took Dynamic Assertives such as Rachel Carson and others to forge the paradigm change that made environmentalism an acceptable mainstream stance in this country (retrograde radio-talk-show hosts notwithstanding).

Dynamic Assertives differ from Dynamic Aggressives in that the former serve as catalysts for change without seeking to control other people. They are opinion-makers who can look beyond themselves to the common good, but their mission is to inspire and motivate other people, not to gain power over them. So Dynamic Aggressives lead mainly by sharing ideas that others can use. Gandhi is an excellent example. He did not want to control other people, nor did he ask the rest of the world to live as he did. Through his own evolution as a human being, he simply showed others that change was possible. He chose to provide a model for society, not to run it. By the way, Gandhi is also an example of the fact that you don't have to be outgoing to be a Dynamic Assertive. You can be a quiet person. Mind power does not require high-volume projection to make itself felt.

More than any other energy type, Dynamic Assertives live in the moment. They are spontaneous and fluid people who respond to their circumstances. If they like something, it shows. If they dislike something, that also shows, and they don't pretend to be engaged in something when they're not. They may be lighthearted one moment and serious the next. In addition, they have a childlike curiosity that leads them to explore all aspects of life, so they would be the first to go to the moon or the bottom of the ocean.

The Dynamic Assertive's disregard for limitations is one of his or her most distinctive qualities. Whereas others might view fear, failure, or adversity as insurmountable roadblocks in life, the Dynamic Assertive views these as challenges. It's not that this group doesn't have fears, but rather that they face those fears and go through them. When Dynamic Assertives make mistakes—and they do so plenty of times—they pick themselves up and go on with their lives. Failure and disappointment become a part of their lifelong learning process rather than reasons to abandon their dreams.

The joy of creating often outweighs the adversity a Dynamic Assertive may face. Consider George Washington Carver, who overcame slavery and racism in the South to develop into a self-educated man and become one of this country's most important horticultural scientists and inventors. He created new uses for peanuts, sweet potatoes, and soy plants, which he helped develop in the South, where the soil had been increasingly depleted from overcultivation of cotton and tobacco. His work ended up providing a big boost for the economy of the region, and Carver went on to become the head of the agriculture department at Tuskegee Institute in Alabama, where he instituted a "school on wheels" that traveled around the state to teach farmers the principles of soil enrichment. He was a true Dynamic Assertive manifesting the high side of his energy; he had the talent, intelligence, and charisma to transcend immense society-imposed handicaps.

A problem Dynamic Assertives may have is that of being misunderstood by others. One reason is that, as intellectually honest people, they reveal their true reactions to things. So when they like something, they tend to show it, and when they dislike something, they show it too. There's no equivocation; you don't have to second-guess them. But this makes a lot of people nervous because it goes against the social convention of being falsely agreeable. This is especially so in the case of women, who are generally expected to be polite dissemblers in the cause of pleasing others. So Dynamic Assertives can be called rude or uncaring when in fact they're just trying to be up-front with people.

They can also be called just plain weird! And they *are* different in that this is a very inner-directed group. We have to respect the fact that any time we're in the presence of someone who is very charismatic and intellectually strong, he is not going to be functioning in the same way that most people around him are. For instance, a Dynamic Assertive may be very quiet and calm when everyone else is excited. Or he may be very excited when other people are calm. He doesn't act based on how everyone else is acting. He acts based on how he feels at the moment—and is therefore labeled strange. (By the way, substitute *she* for *he* in this paragraph to get a feeling for how women Dynamic Assertives may have an even harder time being accepted than men!)

An interesting aspect of Dynamic Assertives is that they tend to be less limited by the aging process than other people are. First of all, as independent thinkers, they don't buy into how a person is "supposed to" act at any particular age. Second, they're just not interested in slowing down for one second. I know some Dynamic Assertives who are in their eighties. When you're with them, you forget immediately that you're dealing with octogenarians. Whereas another person may have only their youth, looks, and body to excite someone, these people have far and away more than that. They have a dynamic, high-velocity energy to share, and that's not an age-dependent gift.

In short, members of this energy group are the most exciting to be around. They've got the vision and drive of the Dynamic Aggressives, but without that group's need for control, they're generally more generous and—to use a plain word but one that says it—they're generally nicer. And their intellect-generated charisma can be such a magnetic force that you remember time spent with a Dynamic Assertive your whole life.

FROM IDEALISM TO HEDONISM: THE UP AND DOWN SIDES OF DYNAMIC ASSERTIVES

From the high end to the low end of a Dynamic Assertive's energy there's a big swing, and some people in this group do go to each extreme during their lives, sometimes repeatedly. Dynamic Assertives have the potential for high-end qualities such as selflessness and compassion, and they also have the potential for self-absorption and an egotistical perspective. When they get distracted from the ideals that give meaning to their lives, they may lose their focus on constructive change and become self-destructive.

On the up side, Dynamic Assertives have the patience to listen to others and see issues from their viewpoint. But they lose that essential balance on their down side. Then they may become self-righteous and attempt to persuade others that their beliefs are the only correct ones. And they can be highly successful at this endeavor! People who interact with a Dynamic Assertive must take care to evaluate the validity of their belief systems, because sometimes charisma can lead them down the wrong path.

Ascending their energy curve, Dynamic Assertives can be exceptionally giving and compassionate; they express their heart energy better than any other type of person. But on their down side, when their vision narrows and they become self-centered, compassion disappears. Dynamic Assertives can become selfish and full of pride; they may exaggerate their own importance to generate attention.

When Dynamic Assertives pursue their beliefs, they can become overzealous and compulsive. In some cases they no longer share their ideas constructively with society because their manner puts people off. They may cease to communicate in a balanced and reasonable way that allows other people to understand their message. Or they become like racehorses going at breakneck speed; other people can't keep up and eventually become exhausted by the effort. And the Dynamic Assertive himself can burn out.

In fact, Dynamic Assertives must be especially attuned to the need for balance in life. They can become such workaholics that they deny other vital aspects of living, such as developing their relationships, health, and spirituality. They may surround themselves with a lot of parasitic people and meaningless activities, such as partying and entertaining, to compensate for a mounting sense of insecurity and loneliness. And, sadly, they may abandon their pursuit of ideals for the pursuit of material wealth.

But such greed isn't the rule. In general I've found that the most generous people in the world are Dynamic Assertives, and if this generosity is not taken too far, it is definitely an up-side trait. There are a couple of reasons that Dynamic Assertives are so generous. One is that they usually don't have problems making money. However, even when they are living quite modestly, Dynamic Assertives will often be extremely magnanimous with what they do have. You see, money and possessions are not the be-all and end-all for Dynamic Assertives; this group is much less status-conscious than Dynamic Aggressives. The be-all and end-all for Dynamic Assertives is *ideas*, which they like to share—and so their things, and even their homes, just kind of become part and parcel of the sharing process. This is the second reason Dynamic Assertives are often so magnanimous: To them, mind and spirit supersede the material. You might even say that, to a Dynamic Assertive, the material is immaterial!

An amazing level of hospitality may be part of the Dynamic Assertive's magnanimity. They make it extremely easy for you to be in their environment. In fact, in the case of some Dynamic Assertives I know, their house is basically an open house—a place where you, and many other friends, too, are free to just *be*. There's no constricting "guest" feeling in their homes because you're not really a guest—you're a participant in the experience of life that you and your Dynamic Assertive friend are sharing. The phrase "My house is your house" rings very true when you're in the home of many a Dynamic Assertive.

This up-side picture of Dynamic Assertive generosity is a beautiful one, but of course there can be problems with it—big problems. For one, sometimes a Dynamic Assertive won't be financially well off, and yet he'll continue to—almost literally—give friends the shirt off his back, and severely impoverish himself in the process. For another thing, friends who are not of the same energy group just don't have it in them to reciprocate at the Dynamic Assertive's level of generosity, and if the Dynamic Assertive expects this, he or she may at some point become quite disappointed and hurt.

Third, even if a Dynamic Assertive isn't financially wiped out by being overly generous, he or she is prone to being egregiously used. A Dynamic Assertive friend of mine falls into this category. He's got a large house that's forever filled with guests. But what are some of these "friends" doing? They're making long-distance phone calls from his house for hours on end and not paying for them. They're eating meal after free meal at his table and never offering to cook, much less pay. They're even stealing things out of his rooms. I've tried to tell him that his generosity has gone from an up-side trait to a problem, but sometimes one Dynamic Assertive talking to another has trouble getting through!

Dynamic Assertives on their up side are quite capable of relaxing, unlike their energy cousins the Dynamic Aggressives, who don't know how to rest. This facility in the art of relaxation is a big plus in terms of health. On the down side in the health area, Dynamic Assertives, when they are manifesting their energy at its lowest level, can lose control—and fast. The respect they have for their minds and bodies on the high end may simply disappear. If they are not careful, they can become highly self-destructive and hedonistic, often developing addictions to junk food, alcohol, and drugs, as well as gambling. Their bodies may become polluted, increasing their susceptibility to disease. This begins a downward spiral, and a Dynamic Assertive can become mentally and physically ill very quickly on the down side.

A difference between a down-side Dynamic Assertive and a down-side Dynamic Aggressive is that the former tends not to destroy other people, but rather himself or herself. The damage is directed inward, although, of course, those who are very close to a downward-spiraling Dynamic Assertive would be negatively affected as well.

UNDERSTAND, CONCEPTUALIZE, LEAD: THE WORK OF DYNAMIC ASSERTIVES

Dynamic Assertives are highly functioning people when they operate from the high side of their energy. Place them in any new environment, and their first impulse is to organize it and make it work. Note: They don't have to own it or preside over it. But they do have a keen sense of order and can envision the best way to make a place or a situation function well.

One of the distinguishing characteristics of the Dynamic energies is that they are conceptually creative.

Dynamic Assertives, in particular, love to bring their new ideas to fruition. They're certainly not the type to sit around and let good ideas slip by. They take advantage of every opportunity to turn their ideas into reality, enthusiastically explaining to others what they're up to and how others can help.

Dynamic Assertives generally do not focus on personal achievement goals. For them, the point of any endeavor—and of life, for that matter—is not to win or to gain control, as in the case of Dynamic Aggressives, but to arrive at new levels of understanding. As a result, they believe the process is the key. Dynamic Assertives are motivated to explore the processes of their lives. This orientation also applies to their work and to their interactions with others. The Dynamic Assertive is a systems person who designs solutions to problems and determines how a job should be done. At that point, he or she often turns the project over to other energy types, such as Creative Assertives, to devise the actual mechanics, and Adaptive Aggressives, to see that the work is implemented.

Sometimes Dynamic Assertives will have Adaptive Supportives working for them—which is fine—but will expect them to perform in a visionary or creative way, and then become disappointed when they don't. I've seen this happen with several of my friends who are Dynamic Assertives; they end up yelling at people in their offices because these workers are not thinking along the same lines they are. It's unfair, and Dynamic Assertives have to guard against such unrealistic expectations.

Dynamic Assertives often like to work for themselves. In this way they can pursue the issues that have meaning to them and maintain responsibility for their own lives. Given their sense of independence, Dynamic Assertives generally do not fit into established institutions, which can make them feel constrained and controlled.

Dynamic Assertives have tremendous raw energy, and sometimes it seems as if they do in a week what others people might do in a year, or even a lifetime. But while all this get-up-and-go is commendable, sometimes sit-down-and-stop is a good thing, too, and Dynamic Assertives often forget this. They'll work twenty hours a day without setting aside time to rest their minds and bodies. Another pitfall: Dynamic Assertives can be highly critical of themselves and others. Perfectionism, in that it demands the highest level of performance from oneself and one's assistants, can be a good thing. But the down side of perfectionism is that one can become opinionated, judgmental, and intolerant of other people's weaknesses.

Dynamic Assertives can swing between cooperation at one end of the spectrum and competitiveness at the other. When they are ascending their energy curve, they will work in harmony with others to actualize a vision. But they may become competitive with other Dynamic Assertives and, on the low end, this competition may result in unnecessary rivalry. In extreme cases, Dynamic Assertives will become territorial, protecting their turf by negating the accomplishments of others.

Beyond that, Dynamic Assertives must be constantly aware of the potential for spiritual burnout. All of us can identify people who had wonderful ideas to share and who could have made a great difference in the lives of others. But if their ideas are not accepted—always a danger for Dynamic Assertives because others misun-

63

derstand them—they can become disillusioned and bitter. Why do they have a gift, they ask, if others will not accept it? This question cannot be answered intellectually, and Dynamic Assertives must turn to the spiritual realm to put such disappointments in perspective.

Success is important to Dynamic Assertives because it validates their beliefs and ideals. They want other people to accept their ideas and respond to their creations; thus they measure their success according to that acceptance. But they may come to resent the things that accompany success—the many people in their lives, the demands of the public—or they may become arrogant. As for the monetary aspect of success, on the high end, money does not define the lives of this group or play a significant role in motivating them. Many Dynamic Assertives make a lot of money and spend it just as easily. They generally are not the type to play the stock market or otherwise invest their money. They would rather spend it on living. The down side is that Dynamic Assertives may use their money totally selfishly, rather than support charities or other causes that go beyond themselves.

Despite all the problems that Dynamic Assertives can have vis à vis the world of work, when they do make their mark, theirs are the most meaningful and inspiring contributions. I'll give you a good example; the Dynamic Assertive in question is someone I've had the privilege to know, Bob Guccione. Yes, he's the editor of *Penthouse Magazine*, but he's an unsung Dynamic Assertive hero, as far as I'm concerned. I'll tell you why.

Several years ago I had written an article on the politics of cancer, the first major article of its type in America. Back then, nobody in any major medium would take on the cancer establishment. A tiny newspaper called *Our Town* did publish that first article, though, and then an editor at *Forum* magazine, Al Freedman, a longtime friend of Guccione, read the article and called me. "Why don't you meet Bob Guccione?," he said.

I didn't know either of them, and I'd never read *Penthouse,* but we set up an appointment and I went over to meet Bob.

He turned out to be a very soft-spoken, quiet man. But this is what he said: "I like what you're doing and I like what it means. I'm going to help you and I'm going to take your articles and put them into my publication so sixteen million people can read them." And that was the end of the meeting.

Then, a week later, there was another meeting, but this time, all of the lawyers, editors, salespeople, and everyone else from *Penthouse* was there. And every one of them was coming down against the articles. "We're going to have lawsuits; we can't defend ourselves against the lawsuits. Sponsors are going to withdraw their ads because these multinational corporations, including drug cartels, own all kinds of advertisers that we use in our publication." Everyone was dead set against the articles.

But Guccione said to me and to the whole group, "If I have to go without a single advertiser and take every nickel to put this out, I'm going to do it. If I lose 20 million dollars an issue, I'll lose it." He said, "We're going to save some lives and we're going to take on the cancer establishment. That's my promise." The man was going against the advice of his entire staff.

Here was an example of an inner-directed man who believed in a cause and then acted on it. He believed in taking on authority, and he was a man who was fiercely independent and autonomous. Yes, he also promoted sexuality and freedom of sexual expression; he promoted erotic fantasy fulfillment. This was within his rights, and part of the needs of other people.

But when it came to social commitment, he was more determined than any other person I've ever met in the United States, and he took people on while incurring a tremendous potential for loss. He really could have lost it all. As it turned out, he did lose a lot. You see, he did print the articles, and he offered free article reprints to anyone who objected to his magazine, so that they wouldn't have to buy it to get the information. But then 1.3 million free reprints were given out. Also, he lost about seven pages' worth of advertisements, which meant that he lost, over a period of a year, probably 11 million dollars. Now, what kind of person would willingly give up 11 million dollars to have an article or series of articles published?

A Dynamic Assertive would. Many people over the years have requested reprints of or have been affected by those articles. They've no doubt saved a lot of lives and changed a lot of lives, but none of this would have happened without the dynamism of Bob Guccione.

RELATIONSHIPS—FOR THE HERE AND NOW

The Dynamic Assertive's first relationship is with life. This group wants to experience all that life has to offer, and so living—not relating to one other person on a

daily basis—is the priority. Consequently their relationships tend to be measured; Dynamic Assertives may
share certain aspects of their life or a certain amount of
time with a partner. They generally do not form the all-
encompassing, long-lasting type of relationship that society has stamped with approval. Once again they are
not comfortable with the mold our culture has cast.

For most people, the idea of having measured relationships is an alien concept. You're either in a relationship every day, or you're not in it at all. But Dynamic
Assertives have a more fluid sense of life. They generally do not value permanency as much as the ability to
live in the moment. Thus they can share time with someone one day but not see the person at all the next. Given
their highly independent nature, they're happy to be
loners at times and they simply do not have the same
need for permanent relationships that other people do.
This can be a real problem because, since Dynamic Assertives are exceptionally magnetic, people tend to *want*
to have a permanent relationship with them. But wanting won't necessarily make something happen when it
goes against a person's natural life energy. So if you
happen to be in a relationship with a Dynamic Assertive, remember: It's not going to be always, and you're
not always going to come first. It's nothing personal,
though!

Compared to other energy types, Dynamic Assertives
are more discriminating in the relationships they form.
They look for people who are enjoyable to be with but
who are similarly independent and open-ended in their
approach to relationships. They can be supportive of
others but also impatient. They don't want to be a care-

taker for someone who is merely trying to cope with life, as opposed to experiencing it to its fullest.

Dynamic Assertives are spontaneous; they do whatever comes to mind. If there's anything that will unsettle them, it's a person who attempts to regulate their lives by setting boundaries in a relationship. So again, if you're in a relationship with a Dynamic Assertive, it's nothing personal, but they're not going to take well to your trying to rein them in with restrictions. Think of having a relationship with a Dynamic Assertive as being along for the ride. It can be a real joyride, but you're not going to be too popular if you keep putting on the brakes.

More than any other energy type, Dynamic Assertives have a difficult time being monogamous. They can be fiercely loyal, dedicated, and sensitive to the people in their lives, but they generally recognize that one person cannot meet all of their needs. What's more, they want to dedicate their energy to the life process, not to maintaining a relationship within the narrow framework that most people set. The confines of a monogamous relationship can make them feel bored, frustrated, and angry. And ultimately their spouses are likely to end up angry, too. I'd say that if you're looking for a picture-book, long-term romance, complete with country cottage and white picket fence, a Dynamic Assertive is not the way to go. There are other energies better suited to live happily ever after behind that fence.

Dynamic Assertives tend to have a lot of people coming into and out of their lives. Their natural charisma and constructive energy attract people who want to share in the excitement, and Dynamic Assertives can have hundreds of acquaintances and friends with whom they interact regularly; they feel comfortable with many different types of relationships and levels of sharing. A problem comes sometimes, though, with juggling these multiple relationships and finding time to spend with the people who are most important to them. Some of these people, wanting more, will get tired of waiting for the Dynamic Assertive to get around to them, and will drop from the scene. This contributes to the high turnover rate in the Dynamic Assertive's social circle.

Most Dynamic Assertives have no interest in controlling other people. But if they are not careful, they may influence others unduly without realizing they have done so. The danger is that another person will become dependent on the Dynamic Assertive, and he or she may feel suffocated and bogged down by the relationship. To protect themselves from this scenario, Dynamic Assertives often seem to keep others at a slight distance.

Dynamic Assertives are especially wary of insecure people. Since they don't feel possessive of their partners and friends, they expect the same in return. When a Dynamic Assertive becomes involved with someone who is jealous, there's likely to be a great deal of conflict. Undoubtedly the other person will feel threatened by all the activity and people in the Dynamic Assertive's life. Many Dynamic Assertives respond to this jealousy by ending their other relationships with friends. But this stopgap measure, intended to keep the peace, is hardly a healthy or a satisfying way to handle the problem. If a Dynamic Assertive must deny his or her natural energy to appease the jealousy of another, then the value of the relationship is questionable.

I've seen this jealousy situation happen. I had a male friend who was one of the finest Dynamic Assertives

I've ever met. He was the type who was up for anything. He would, for instance, call you up out of the blue
and say, "Let's go to the museum!" and you would get
there and somehow find yourself eight floors below
ground level looking at the priceless manuscripts the
museum had in storage. I'm still not sure how that one
happened, but that was the kind of zany outing that was
his style.

Anyway, my friend married an Adaptive Aggressive
who was very threatened by his other relationships; she
asked him to give all that up so that they would have
only "safe" couples relationships.

He complied; the noncouples, spontaneous activities
were gone from his life. But the pizzazz was also gone
from his life, which became a deflated, tamed, comfort-
seeking thing. There were no more spur-of-the-moment
adventures, just living-room, married-couples socializing.

I think we all know—regardless of our energy
group—that these socially acceptable couples relationships can be excruciatingly boring. I mean, face it: Four
people being mutually interesting to each other is a condition that's almost impossible to fulfill. And for the
fast-paced, mind-driven Dynamic Assertive, an entire
evening of Mr. and Mrs. Smith plus Mr. and Mrs.
Jones—well, let's just say that this is not likely to be his
or her favorite activity! My friend didn't complain, but
in my book he lost a lot—too much, in fact, considering
his extreme Dynamic Assertive nature.

More than any other energy type, Dynamic Assertives
need time alone for introspection, away from their relationships with friends and partners. For most of their
waking hours, they give an enormous amount of their

energy to other people. In a sense, society runs off the energy that Dynamic Assertives provide. But periodically they have to withdraw from society and give themselves time to re-energize if they're to keep giving at the same level. When they do withdraw, others should understand that they're doing so out of personal necessity, not out of unfriendliness.

As fluid, spontaneous types, Dynamic Assertives are not the most predictable of folk. This can be upsetting to others attempting to have a relationship with members of this energy group. Unpredictability is a paradox. People are attracted by it, but they're also put off by it. Unpredictable people are like firecrackers—you don't know if you really want to play with them all the time.

It's worth noting that Dynamic Assertive women face particular problems in forming relationships. These women have all the same qualities as their male counterparts—they're intelligent, challenging, and highly engaged with life, which makes them threatening to the average man. A Dynamic Assertive woman has to be an equal in any relationship, and she must find a partner who is not threatened by her charisma and self-assuredness. That's no easy task, and many Dynamic Assertive women end up with partners who try to prove that they are superior by competing with them, often in childish ways.

As a result, many Dynamic Assertive women find that their relationships are draining, or even impossible to sustain. Some men simply won't accept these women for who they are and attempt to "tame" them by bringing their energy under control. For example, a Dynamic Assertive's partner may want her to downplay her career. But, of course, trying to suppress a Dynamic Assertive's energies is not going to make for a good relationship in the long run.

Despite their problems with romantic relationships, Dynamic Assertives can be terrific friends. They are extremely loyal; they never forget a friend, and will go to great lengths to help the people they care about. One Dynamic Assertive I know was in England when he heard that a man who had worked for him fifteen years earlier was dying of cancer in the United States. The Dynamic Assertive did not have any money, but he used his credit cards to fly to Miami, that same night, to visit the man. That type of loyalty and sensitivity is typical of Dynamic Assertives on the high side of their energy.

As parents, Dynamic Assertives may not be so successful. Parenting a young child requires constancy—not often the Dynamic Assertive's strong point. But when they are in touch with the higher self, they can do an excellent job in some aspects of child rearing. For example, they will encourage independent thought in a child and share all their insight about human nature—both highly valuable gifts to the young. And they tend to speak to their children with respect. This is an idea that does not seem to have occurred to some people in our society, but Dynamic Assertives usually respect the mental and spiritual potential of others, regardless of age—and even of species; members of this energy group can be true friends of animals. On the down side, however, Dynamic Assertive parents can be so self-absorbed and impatient that they distance a child. Even worse, they may fail to devote time alone with the child—a cardinal sin of parenthood—because they are so preoccupied with their work and the other people in their lives. If the child must compete with throngs of people for the parent's attention, he or she will resent it mightily.

Energy Combinations

To form healthy relationships, Dynamic Assertives must be given the freedom to be who they are. The energy types most likely to create this space are Creative Assertives, other Dynamic Assertives, and Dynamic Supportives, provided they are operating from the high side of their energy. These people understand the Dynamic Assertive's devotion to the life process, while other types may not be able to tolerate it.

A Dynamic Assertive and a Creative Assertive can make a beautiful combination, especially when both are ascending their energy curve. They can forge a wonderful, trusting relationship that allows for an exciting exchange of ideas. The Dynamic Assertive sees the big picture; the Creative Assertive knows how to execute the details to complete that picture. Because they are caring and sensitive people, Creative Assertives will be cooperative and supportive of a Dynamic Assertive. They will make sacrifices to help bring the Dynamic Assertive's vision to life and benefit other people.

Two Dynamic Assertives also can have a spectacular relationship. If both are on their up side, they will share their strengths and their love of life, creating an exciting and spontaneous relationship. It's like two meteors traveling side by side: They brighten the sky wherever they go. The beauty of this relationship is that both will be living and sharing in the moment; the relationship doesn't anticipate tomorrow, or seek to set boundaries, or attempt to establish a permanent commitment. It simply allows the passion of the moment to exist without looking to define and encode it.

Two Dynamic Assertives can have a good business relationship as well, as long as they avoid the natural tendency to compete. They can accomplish a lot together and even help to pace each other so that neither one burns out. For the relationship to work, though, each Dynamic Assertive has to respect the other and recognize that the relationship has its limitations—the fact that they are business partners does not mean that they can meddle in the other's personal sphere.

One of the finest friendships possible for a Dynamic Assertive is with a Dynamic Supportive. They have a lot in common—their high level of energy, love of life, and creativity, for example—but they won't feel the constant need to compete and prove themselves to one another. It would be an easy and highly enjoyable relationship for both.

A relationship with an Adaptive Aggressive is trickier. It could be fine if the Adaptive Aggressive does not have ulterior motives. The Adaptive Aggressive may be quite effective in implementing the Dynamic Assertive's vision, and the two may genuinely enjoy being together as well, appreciating each other's very different types of energy and ways of interacting with the world. But there can be problems. Given their opportunistic nature, Adaptive Aggressives may join with a Dynamic energy to better their own condition or to learn what they can from the Dynamic Assertive before moving on. What's more, the Adaptive Aggressive might attempt to tie up the relationship by establishing boundaries for the Dynamic Assertive, something the Dynamic Assertive will come to resent.

Another danger is that an Adaptive Aggressive will assume all the qualities of a Dynamic Assertive—his or her openness, assertiveness, and experimental approach to life—to appear to be just the right person for the Dynamic Assertive. This mimicry is a specialty of the Adaptive Aggressive, and it can be appealing to Dynamic Assertives who are looking for someone to agree with them, compliment them, and do what they want to do. Think of Elvis Presley, a Dynamic Assertive who surrounded himself with Adaptive Aggressives. These people spent more time feeding off his stardom than providing him with true friendship.

With this type of relationship, the Dynamic Assertive is not dealing with the Adaptive Aggressive's real self. The Dynamic Assertive may do certain things for the pure joy of it, while the Adaptive Aggressive is merely configuring himself or herself, chameleonlike, to the present environment because he or she expects to gain something from it in the end. In this case, the relationship between a Dynamic Assertive and an Adaptive Aggressive can turn explosive.

Danger: The Betrayal Trap

A disturbing phenomenon I've seen too much of lately is the tell-all book, in which an Adaptive type who's been trusted by and living or working with a Dynamic Assertive turns around and writes an unflattering book about him or her. This is the in-print manifestation of the problem of betrayal that Dynamic Assertives often face.

Dynamic Assertives are particularly prone to this backstabbing phenomenon because of the kind of lives they lead and the kind of people they are. Both Dynamic Aggressives and Dynamic Assertives lead unusual lives and accomplish extraordinary things that others like to hear or read about. And both groups depend on many people around them to implement the details of their work. But Dynamic Assertives, who tend to be the more forward-thinking and unconventional of these two energy groups, as well as the less cagey, can supply a potential bad-mouther with more material. What's more, Dynamic Assertives' tendency to share—everything from ideas to feelings to their means of sustenance and shelter—means that others can really get involved in their lives. Then, if these others are less than scrupulous, they can use what they've learned to make a profit, or simply to create gossip or bad feeling. So Dynamic Assertives should always be on guard against the danger of betrayal, although for those living a fully engaged life, being betrayed at some point is probably inevitable.

OPENNESS TO PERSONAL CHANGE

Dynamic Assertives have a tremendous potential for growth. Unlike some of the other energy types, they thrive on change and take a fearless approach to achieving it in their lives.

Personal growth is always based on self-knowledge, and one thing that can be strongly said about Dynamic

Assertives is that they know who they are. Introspective souls, they've spent hours pondering themselves, their ethics, and their places and missions in the world. They're not generally religious but they are spiritual, certainly in the sense that their own spirit is known to them, having been examined so closely and so often. Other energy types, without a similar feeling for their own personal core, can fall prey to following false or dangerous gurus. A radio demagogue or shock jock, for instance, or a TV evangelist, can provide an attractive, ready-made belief package to those who, lacking their own sense of identity, need one to latch on to. But Dynamic Assertives don't fall into this category; in fact, they're often the ones who point out to others the foolishness of being a sheeplike follower.

Dynamic Assertives have an innate sense of what it takes to grow; they recognize that growth is possible only when one is vulnerable. Vulnerability leads to openness, spontaneity, and fluidity, all of which provide fertile ground for positive change. Because Dynamic Assertives are willing to live in the moment, they can turn on a dime and take advantage of opportunities to change, and to have peak experiences in the process.

The best example of this ability of Dynamic Assertives to "go with the flow" and opportunistically learn from the experience is their perspective on failure. Dynamic Assertives can fail time and again without allowing failure to break their resolve. When they fall down they simply pick themselves up again. They don't revel in the pain of the fall, and they certainly don't listen to naysayers who advise people to back off and play it safe once they fail. The Dynamic Assertive uses failure as a

77

tool for learning, at times turning negatives to positives in an amazing way.

One obstacle to growth for Dynamic Assertives is their childhood conditioning. Many Dynamic Assertives feel conflicted throughout life because they were conditioned to be another energy type, such as an Adaptive Supportive. They may get a lot of negative input during childhood from parents who do not understand their Assertive energy and who squelch their dreams. As they become adults, they sense that their life is not as fulfilling as it should be, but they are terrified of allowing their true self to shine through.

When a Dynamic Assertive's early conditioning exerts a negative influence on his or her life, it's something like gravity pulling at an ascending star. And in fact at any point in life, they can be in danger of being pulled back into the conformist world by someone who expects them to fit into society's mold—to take a nine-to-five job, perhaps, or to form a permanent relationship that requires them to deny vital aspects of their natural energy.

The Dynamic Assertive woman, in particular, may have strong conditioning to be an Adaptive Supportive; indeed, women are rarely conditioned to be a Dynamic energy of any type. As a result, they may have to go against the grain their entire lives, fighting to overcome people's perceptions of who they should be and how they should live their lives. And even those who overcome this obstacle to express their true energy may face another problem. Given their strength, individuality, and high level of functioning in relation to others, there may be very little impetus for them to grow. Some of them get caught in a circular pattern of growth, focusing all their energy on one area of interest until they conquer it and become bored. In the process, they fail to identify and explore other avenues of growth and transformation.

DYNAMIC ASSERTIVES AND THE NEED FOR RENEWAL

More than anything, members of this energy group need to establish a balance in their lives. They can't run at full speed for long periods of time, pursuing the process of life and their visions relentlessly, without taking time out for introspection. Remember, if you are a Dynamic Assertive, your charisma will draw many people to you, but if you're the type who just "cain't say 'no,' " you're going to be surrounded by such a mob all the time that the people whom you really care about will not be able to get through to you, and they'll eventually be repelled. Also, you can unwittingly repel people with your potential for self-absorption and self-destructive behavior.

To balance your energy and use it constructively, you need to clear some space in your life for meditation and reflection. Give yourself a chance to renew, and you will have the fuel to manifest your energy at its highest level. Many Dynamic Assertives lose this ability because they allow themselves to become perpetually busy. They get so carried away by their own creativity and energy that they create a terrible imbalance in their lives. If you work so hard—even at something you truly enjoy—that you deny other aspects of living, you will alter your perception of life and your ability to relate to others.

The danger, then, is that you will forget to plant the seeds of growth in your life, allowing yourself instead to be consumed by work, by overexpansion, and by the many conflicts that pepper our day-to-day existence. Learn to delegate authority so you have time to renew, and learn to be patient with others who have their own pace and approach to completing a project.

Remember that there are negative consequences to a self-sacrificing commitment to any cause, no matter how worthy. If you are not careful, you can develop a "martyr complex" that ultimately makes you self-obsessive, overly intense, and boring. This can kill your spontaneity, joy, and creativity—the driving forces in your life.

Be aware, too, of the tendency to pursue new projects for the wrong reasons. Perhaps you are just chasing money or trying to prove yourself to other people. Be sure to pull back from time to time to check your motives and avoid these traps. These are the times when you can say, "I don't need more money right now. I don't need to compete with others by starting another project. What I need is to reflect on my deeds and allow myself to grow." If you "declutter" your workload in this way from time to time, the work you do take on will be more rewarding.

A final challenge: Be more selective in the people you bring into your life. Like many Dynamic Assertives, you probably have a tendency to form dozens of relationships that have no real meaning. They may simply be byproducts of the constant activity in your life, not a recognition by both parties that you have something to share. Such relationships can be draining, and they take time away from those that really are important in your life. Again, declutter, and give your best qualities a chance to shine.

THE BRIDGE BETWEEN ENERGIES: DYNAMIC SUPPORTIVES

It takes a while to appreciate some people, but if you meet someone who's immediately likable, there's a good chance that she or he is a Dynamic Supportive. People with this energy have a genuine affability that comes through right away, making them instantly easy to relate to. What's more, they can relate to all different types of people. While a high-powered Dynamic Aggressive might have nothing to say to a down-to-earth Adaptive Supportive, or a Creative Assertive, on a bad day, might have nothing to say to anyone, the Dynamic Supportive usually can communicate on a positive level with everyone. You could say that, like the sun, he casts warmth on all people, without regard to group or status.

Indeed, Dynamic Supportives are particularly warm-hearted. This compassionate, charismatic group includes many healers, conciliators, teachers, and clergy. Dynamic Supportives have stability, an energetic balance, and an inner sense of what is genuine. Other people are drawn to them, but Dynamic Supportives are not oriented toward making changes in others or in their environment. They do have a definite set of values, but they do not force these on anyone. Instead they quietly set standards by their actions, warmth, and presence. In other words, they motivate others by example.

Dynamic Supportives are sensitive to the emotional energies of their environment. They are energetically and intuitively attuned to other people, and they naturally engage on an emotional level. They have an empathetic nature, which means that they identify more easily than others do with what they see or contemplate, becoming, at the extreme, like sponges for whatever vibrations surround them. They have inner vision, and they sense the broad schemes of nature. Dynamic Supportives are independent people who have a strong will and character and an especially strong sense of self. Other people and situations do not intimidate them.

On their up side, Dynamic Supportives establish a healthy psychic coming and going as they connect emphatically with the external world and as they return home to the self. On their down side, they may absorb outside conflicts and feel troubled, unbalanced, and physically ill. Their distress and concern for other people can cause them to lose sight of their own plans, and they forget to take care of themselves.

Many Dynamic Supportives might be considered "unfocused dynamics" because they have a lot of charisma but do not necessarily know where or how to use it. They may meander in life and fail to actualize their abundant potential. In many cases, in fact, they can be unmotivated, lethargic, and even lazy in realizing their full potential.

This tendency can be enormously frustrating for other people who recognize the untapped potential in a Dynamic Supportive. Imagine Fred Astaire deciding not to pursue a film career because he thinks no one really wants to see him dance anyway, or Einstein deciding not to solve the puzzles of the universe because it's too much hassle. That's the kind of situation the people around a Dynamic Supportive sometimes perceive, and it can drive them crazy. But all the cajoling, prodding, and encouragement in the world won't change the basic nature of the Dynamic Supportive.

When others try to force a Dynamic Supportive to realize his or her potential, it's like blowing up a balloon halfway and then expecting it to continue on its own. It simply won't happen, The balloon deflates again because it is not self-starting. That's why other people must accept that a Dynamic Supportive's potential will be actualized in the context of his or her own life, not according to their own expectations. They have to respect that the Dynamic Supportive is often doing a great deal of good in his or her own way.

Likewise, it would be a mistake to look to the Dynamic Supportive for leadership, as we do with other charismatic people. Dynamic Supportives generally have no interest in directing others. However, they do have a singular ability to bring people together in understanding. Their abilities to view life from a broad perspective and to empathize with others allow them to draw disparate energies into a working whole. They know intuitively what works and what does not. They can facilitate a dialogue in a nonthreatening and non-

85

competitive way. They understand both the Dynamic energies, who typically are the initiators in society, and the Adaptive energies, who help put initiatives into effect. Thus the Dynamic Supportive can serve as a bridge between the two, facilitating communication and cooperation.

Dynamic Supportives sometimes do not take initiative to make social or personal change for several reasons. For one, they are simply content to be who they are. They have nothing to prove to anyone and are not easily externally motivated. Second, they take on the problems of others at their own expense when they do not set limits on their empathy. They can be so drawn into other people's inner conflicts that they live outside themselves psychologically. As they identify with these emotions, their minds may become restless and unfocused. And finally, even though they do plan for the future, Dynamic Supportives can become absorbed in the present. In doing so they adapt to their circumstances, sometimes a little too well. It's not that they don't see the big, long-term picture; they do. But the down side of their seeing the broad picture can be a negative relativism: "Nothing in itself really matters, so why bother?" This gives them an excuse to forget about the details of life and to let things go.

For Dynamic Supportives who want to make personal changes, the tendency to lose focus can be disheartening. As potentially capable planners, they recognize that they have not followed through. They have a tendency to melancholy and may become depressed on their down side. This, in turn, can make it even more difficult for them to keep track of details and to follow through.

The result can be that they find themselves in a negative cycle.

On their up side, Dynamic Supportives have a natural optimism. They are easygoing, joyful, and accepting people. They may have trouble sticking with their long-term plans, but they keep the blues away by doing things for others and making more plans. You can't keep them down. As is the case with the other Dynamic energies, a Dynamic Supportive can experience a major failure in life that would devastate someone else, and yet be back in the game the next day. They approach each endeavor—in both their personal and professional lives—with sincerity and a strong sense of commitment. They are stable, reliable, and extremely responsible in fulfilling their obligations.

Dynamic Supportives are also direct, self-aware, and self-sufficient. If something gets in the way of doing what they believe is right, they address the problem head-on. A Dynamic Supportive will not let personal fears drive his or her life. They don't dance around problems and avoid them; they deal with them directly and face their fears.

While Dynamic Supportives don't back off from their convictions, they do have a softer approach than do other energy types. Their observations and comments are usually relevant and funny because they have a terrific sense of humor. On their up side, they're thoughtful, spontaneous, and unafraid. Part of their charm is that they have a lot of self-confidence, but they don't necessarily do anything earthshaking with it. You won't see them getting into a workaholic rut by slaving away twenty hours a day. In fact, the term "laid back" sometimes seems custom-made for the Dynamic Supportive.

Interestingly, some "Dynamic Supportives" aren't—that is, some people who seem to display Dynamic Supportive energies are not really doing so from a natural inclination, but because of a role inherited from childhood. Many children grow up with caregivers who have not learned to appreciate themselves or who have personal problems with which they cannot cope. When a child is asked to parent the parent—to interpret, facilitate, and keep the peace at home—he or she may later appear to have a natural supportive energy. In some cases this may really be so; in others, the child's conditioned energy may overlay his or her natural energy.

As adults, ostensibly Dynamic Supportive people have to ask themselves if they find joy in the benevolent actions they perform for others. A natural Dynamic Supportive will truly enjoy being helpful and supportive. But the question is tricky, since even the natural Dynamic Supportive may experience stress and depression until he or she has learned to protect the inner self.

A key to identifying false Dynamic Supportives is this: They seek out the helping role more than they are asked to take it on. Natural Dynamic Supportives are sought out, and they tend to be more effective than the next person in motivating and helping others precisely because people are drawn to their charisma, and ask for their help. Also, unlike conditioned Dynamic Supportives, people who are naturally of this life energy do not feel lost or without purpose when they are not functioning in a helping role.

STRONG, GENTLE, ACCOMMODATING . . . *TOO* ACCOMMODATING

Dynamic Supportives have a natural balance, but they are so emphatically attuned to their environment that they can easily be drawn outside themselves and into other people's energy. And when these other people are troubled, chaotic, or negative, the Dynamic Supportive's own balance may be upset.

Indeed, this energy group's concern for other people can lead to trouble if it's not tempered by good judgment. Dynamic Supportives are the group with a lot of members who are often just plain "too nice." They may try to help people who will not help themselves, and spend an enormous amount of time doing things for others. As a result, people may take advantage of these "Mr. or Ms. Nice Guys" if they have not learned to set limits on their empathy and recenter themselves.

The other Dynamic energies—the Aggressive and the Assertive—sometimes rub people the wrong way because they can be opinionated, driven, and rude. The Dynamic Supportive, by contrast, is more likable because he is more mellow—more likely to smile, to agree, to be helpful. But herein lies a problematic aspect of the Dynamic Supportive's life. If a person is agreeable and helpful all the time and then one day, for whatever reason, he doesn't agree, or help, those around him have a tendency to resent it.

"Why aren't you helping me?" they ask.

"I ran out of money."

Or, "Why aren't you agreeing with me?"

"I've come to a different conclusion than you have."

"What kind of an excuse is that?"

Indeed, those are no excuses to people who have been spoiled by a Dynamic Supportive's support. They come to expect things from a Dynamic Supportive that they would never expect from anyone else. So people in this energy group have to take psychic protective steps to make sure others don't take them for granted and then act offended when the Dynamic Supportive steps "out of character."

If Dynamic Supportives do not take these protective steps, they are often prone to disease. On the down side, in fact, Dynamic Supportives may use illness as an excuse not to achieve. Their rationale tends to be something like, "I'll be right there just as soon as I'm well." The problem is not that they fake illness. It is that they do not take responsibility for their own lives. They have a hard time saying no to others and giving themselves equal time.

A Dynamic Supportive on the down side can get set up quite easily. Other people see that they are strong but gentle, an appealing combination that makes others latch on to them. They sense the potential and think, "Gee, this person is really going someplace." Chances are, the Dynamic Supportive does not live up to this observation when he or she is on the down side. They can get lazy and not project their energy into anything worthwhile. There is too much being and not enough doing. You can come back ten years later and they haven't even done the dishes. In many cases they simply do not direct themselves.

The Dynamic Supportive's attention to detail also

swings from one extreme to the other, depending on whether they are on the up side or the down side. On the high end, they pride themselves on their ability to handle the details of life. Their home life is organized, with everything in its proper place. If you were to visit their attic, you would find everything neatly sorted, packed, and labeled by date. On their down side, by contrast, their life has no details. All the small things that make up their daily existence seem to slip away. At this point, they don't even know if they have an attic, let alone what's in it.

On the up side, Dynamic Supportives have positive and flexible energy. But their tendency will be to simply accommodate to a situation when they are on the down side; they neither learn from it nor transform it. Still, most Dynamic Supportives are very strong about standing up for the truth. They are responsible people with excellent character, and they would not let another person take the blame for them. In many respects they are models for character development.

HELPERS PAR EXCELLENCE

Dynamic Supportives are well suited for careers that focus on helping others. They have a giving nature, and they love to deal with other people's energies. These traits can make for good therapists, medical doctors, chiropractors, and social workers. All of these occupations require intelligence, intuition, and communication skills, which Dynamic Supportives generally possess.

It's a cliché that when young people just getting out of

college are asked what kind of job they want, they usually say, "I'd like to work with people." But to really work well with people you have to have a certain flexibility, and it's members of this group, the Dynamic Supportives, who have it. They know how to bend. Dynamic Supportives have the wisdom to analyze a situation while fully realizing that there may be several approaches to it. They have the intelligence to decide on a best approach, but they will not force their conclusions on others. They are good listeners, they have a value system, and they think as much with their hearts as with their minds. These qualities, along with their charisma and willingness to help others, make people pay attention to them.

It's interesting to see the flexibility and mellowness of the Dynamic Supportive reflected in his or her habitat. Their houses tend to have that lived-in look that tells you that the housekeeper is more interested in enjoying life than in keeping the art books arrayed just so on the coffee table. In fact, you might not even be able to *see* the coffee table under what's accumulated on top of it—newspapers, coffee cups, take-out menus, toys, and the like. This is not to say that the Dynamic Supportive is always a slob. On the high end, he or she sometimes gets quite organized. But organization and cleanliness are not the driving forces that they are in the lives of, say, Adaptive Assertives.

Because of the Dynamic Supportive's relaxed attitudes, in relation to housekeeping as well as to other areas of life, his is a comfortable house to visit. If the Dynamic Supportive has teenage children, for example, it will probably be his or her house that the neighborhood kids like to hang out in. They'll know they can grab something good from the refrigerator and even put their feet up on the furniture without the parent having a fit. What's more, the visiting kids will probably be able to actually *talk* to the parent in a meaningful way, without any unpleasantness resulting from the kids having dyed their hair pink, failed algebra, or even come from the wrong side of the tracks.

I have a theory that you can tell where a Dynamic Supportive lives by his yard. Take a walk through a middle-class suburban neighborhood. Everybody's got their picket fences crisply painted a blinding white and their lawns neatly mowed and edged. Then you come to a yard that's a little different. Not only is the fence paint yellowing and peeling, but a picket or two is gone. And the lawn—well, it couldn't be edged because it has no edge. It just sort of fades into mud because the Dynamic Supportive hasn't gotten rid of the shade trees and replaced them with tiny specimen trees the way everyone else on the block has. The Dynamic Supportive likes big, shaggy trees the way he or she likes big, shaggy dogs. The trees rain leaves all over the place in the fall, but this doesn't bother the Dynamic Supportive. His neighbors are tempted to hate him, only they know him, and he's too nice to hate.

The thing is, the neighborhood kids love him. Actually, they love his yard. I have a friend I've discussed my yard theory with, and she believes that it's not so much the front yard that identifies the home of a Dynamic Supportive as the backyard. She offers her own backyard as an example, explaining that her husband is a Dynamic Supportive.

When people are over, she reports, and they look out the back windows, they usually ask, "What is that large hole over there? The one with the mud surrounding it and all those old planks crisscrossing it at odd angles?" They can't help asking because it looks as if some sort of explosive device has landed in the back of her yard, blowing apart a wooden picnic table and Adirondack lawn chair in the process, and it seems as if this event has somehow escaped the whole family's notice.

"Oh, that's my son's fort," she has to explain. She has to reassure the guests that there was no explosive device involved; it's simply that her young son likes to dig, and to build, and so her husband (the Dynamic Supportive) has given him a corner of the yard in which to do both to his heart's content, even to the point of sacrificing a couple of pieces of lawn furniture. On closer inspection the guests see that the fort incorporates stray bits of fencing, a beat-up blanket, and some rope, and that it looks like an eight-year-old's paradise. Indeed, other kids are always coming to play in her yard, preferring it to their own well-manicured little versions of Versailles. The point is that, as a Dynamic Supportive, her husband is involved in helping his son develop his interests, and he is independent enough not to care about prevailing suburban standards.

At work as well as at home, Dynamic Supportives tend to be independent. While they may not be assertive with their independence, they do like to work on their own, rather than be supervised. As a result, they can be especially effective salespeople—not the stereotypical obnoxiously aggressive kind, but the kind who knows how to communicate in a more low-key way and really inform and help the customer. They love to get out there and talk and work with people. Other qualities—including their patience and concern for others—make them excellent teachers. Dynamic Supportives are articulate communicators, and they pride themselves on their capacity to teach others. They can develop a bond of trust between the student and themselves.

Members of the clergy tend to be Dynamic Supportives as well. They will sacrifice for others and tackle important issues, as illustrated by clergy in Central and South America who have battled against human rights violations and even been sentenced to jail for helping people find homes in the underground. The same was true during the Vietnam War, when many members of the clergy spoke out against the ethical atrocities of the war.

In an ideal world, all Dynamic Supportives would be considered a resource to be tapped as catalysts to inspire acts of human decency and as arbitrators to help resolve conflict. Not only are they objective, but they can cooperate with anyone under any circumstances to manage a conflict. They are effective in this way because they know how to put their own egos aside and help others save face and even build self-esteem. Their own performance is important only to the extent that they want to do well at something they care about.

And Dynamic Supportives can deliver a superb performance. When they are motivated to do a job, they do it extremely well. What's more, because they are good people, they will often go out of their way to do a good job, putting in extra time for little compensation.

Given their sensitivity, Dynamic Supportives do not like to be criticized, but they will allow it. On their down side, they may lose their motivation to continue working. That's why many Dynamic Supportives cannot actualize their desire to work for themselves, even though they are unhappy without independence.

THE IDEAL—AND UNIVERSAL—FRIEND

Dynamic Supportives develop relationships based on trust, respect, and unconditional love. Their fine qualities—including loyalty, selflessness, and dependability—can make for an excellent relationship. Dynamic Supportives are also insightful. They have an understanding of the person they are with and will look after his or her needs.

Their willingness to sacrifice adds to their appeal as a partner or friend. Dynamic Supportives won't hesitate to give a loved one anything they have. On the up side, they are forthright partners who will show their feelings openly. They do not hold back. They are loving and affectionate—and they're not afraid to demonstrate their emotions, no matter what the consequences.

Their friendships, too, last a lifetime. If you're looking for a friend who will stick with you in good times and bad, the Dynamic Supportive is it. Even on their down side, Dynamic Supportives will remain good, supportive friends. However, they tend not to be spontaneous or in the moment. They are planners who want to know when and how something is going to happen.

A Dynamic Supportive woman can be a wonderful partner and friend. She will be flexible, understanding, patient, and nurturing. Men find Dynamic Supportive women extremely attractive. They are a fountain of wisdom, and they have great strength. Many men value the energy of a Dynamic Supportive woman more than any other energy type because she is stable and nonthreatening. The woman will not bring so many needs into the relationship that the man feels overwhelmed, as if he must be Superman to maintain his standing in the relationship.

Dynamic Supportive women will not be subordinated in a relationship; they require that a partner treat them very much as an equal. Of all the energy types, none is more willing to go out of her way to help others. But they must be appreciated, and they will take it quite personally if their trust and confidence are betrayed. They hurt deeply, more so than others who may be more callous or indifferent. But they are more willing than other types of women to let go of problems.

The Dynamic Supportive woman generally looks for a strong, monogamous relationship. At the same time, she may have many male friends. Due to her giving and understanding nature, she will not want anyone she likes to disappear from her life. In fact, one danger for Dynamic Supportives—females and males alike—is that they may end up in a bad relationship because they do not like to push anyone out of their lives. They do not detach easily, and it may be hard for them to remove someone from their lives once the relationship is formed.

Dynamic Supportive people are intuitive. They might not change the world, but they understand it. They might not change themselves, but they understand who they are. These qualities make them enormously accepting of other people, warts and all. Dynamic Supportives accept their own weaknesses and the failings of others without criticism. They can be the best of friends and partners because they do not demand perfection from everyone around them. More than any other energy type, they are willing to overlook the flaws and negative aspects of their friends and partners.

Dynamic Supportives can be great parents as well. Their tolerance means that they generally give children a lot of unconditional love. They don't place excessive importance on winning or losing, and they have the constancy and wisdom to provide children with guidance. They're also patient, easygoing, and giving; they're the type of parent who actually looks forward to sitting down with the kids to do homework, or to taking them camping. They foster independence in their children, who often manifest an amazing self-sufficiency at an early age. And their children are usually respectful, belying any outwardly outrageous dress.

Within their family, community, and work environment—their three basic orientations—Dynamic Supportives will try to live according to high ideals. They do not tolerate destruction or injustice. They would be the first in a community to rally others to clean up their block or to challenge an unfair practice in the school system. Dynamic Supportives will always confront such issues, but generally with a more tempered passion than some other energy types. Dynamic Supportives are not vengeful people who want to inflict harm on others.

They are also humble and kindhearted. When you're around a Dynamic Supportive, you recognize them by these qualities. Chances are they will not achieve national recognition for their work because they lack the motivation to do so. But they can be counted on to play a vital role in any group or organization to which they belong, providing a vital equilibrium to balance the extremes within the group.

As for energy combinations, a beauty of the Dynamic Supportive is that he or she can blend in with just about anybody. No matter what type of energy they join with, their natural charisma will shine through. Dynamic Supportives are happy people, and other energy types will be drawn to that quality. And whereas other energies may be too intense and self-absorbed, Dynamic Supportives will reach out to relate to all types of people. They are patient and understanding, and their lifestyle is comforting and familiar to others.

To zero in on a particularly promising energy combination, a Dynamic Supportive can have a terrific friendship with a Dynamic Assertive. In fact, this is one of the easiest and most enjoyable of all relationships because both parties understand what it means to have strength. Neither has to compete with or prove anything to the other. It's a hassle-free relationship.

A Dynamic Supportive also can form a permanent and loving relationship with an Adaptive Supportive or a Creative Assertive. The Dynamic Supportive and Adaptive Supportive share a vivacious personality, while the Dynamic Supportive and Creative Assertive have their creativity and intellectual qualities in common.

There is, however, a combination that the Dynamic Supportive should be wary of, and that's a relationship with an Adaptive Aggressive. Given their generosity and kindness, a Dynamic Supportive may be taken advantage of by an Adaptive Aggressive. They could end up doing everything for this person, to their own detriment, if they are not aware of their tendency to put others before themselves.

SEEKING THE SPIRITUAL

For the Dynamic Supportive, emotional and spiritual growth generally supersedes the material. Therefore, transformation is possible for them if they can learn to stay focused and channel their dynamic energy. A positive environment is especially helpful to this energy type. It can make all the difference in a critical period of transition.

When Dynamic Supportives receive unconditional love, they will blossom into strong and unique people. In fact, because they are strong in spirit and character, they tend to blossom no matter what. Unfortunately, many Dynamic Supportives will encounter a spiritual awakening but fail to reach out and grab it. They understand it, but they don't embrace it.

For the Dynamic Supportive, everything is a concept—an idea that does not necessarily have to be actualized. In that context, then, spirituality is just another idea. Dynamic Supportives are moralistic, but they generally are not assertive enough to accept that they can and should live according to a spiritual definition of life.

When the proper conditions exist for their psychospiritual transformation, Dynamic Supportives can become regenerated people, truly joyous and energetic. Their transformation will often have some sort of mystical aspect attached to it. When this group becomes enlightened, their natural intuition and deep vision become enhanced, new energies are released, and they apply their gifts to benevolent service and selfless action.

SET LIMITS, KEEP FOCUSED

If you're a Dynamic Supportive, you face some particular vulnerabilities due to your energy type. Other people may find your capacity for empathy and attunement so pleasing that they encourage you to play a supporting and mirroring role regardless of whether you want to. And you may have an even more difficult time if your parents did not help you set limits as a child and encourage your other identities to take shape. Throughout life you will find again and again that others expect you to provide support, and you may not be able to extricate yourself from this role.

As a Dynamic Supportive you must learn to set limits on these natural inclinations. Otherwise you are susceptible to becoming uncentered, disturbed, and overwhelmed by negative emotional energy in your environment. Your energy may lead you to bond with others on whatever psychological ground is available, even if these other people are involved with inner phantoms, attachments, and complexes. So you can become attached to many types of energy, but your level of stress may increase as you move away from your own and other positive energies. The danger is that you will live too much outside of yourself and then lose track of the way back to tranquillity and balance. Eventually this imbalance may make you vulnerable to disease.

Like many Dynamic Supportives, you may become so

absorbed in other people's energy that you lose sight of your own plans for the future. In a worst-case scenario, this loss of focus will cause distress by combining with the negativity you internalize. At that point you may be susceptible to depression, which means you are even less likely to act on your intentions. A vicious cycle begins.

Learn to set limits on your empathy and to withdraw as needed. The world won't stop turning because you are not there to push it, although people may try to make you think it will. Remember that other people are drawn to the energy of a Dynamic Supportive because they sense his or her strength. They will ask you for help and advice, but you must distinguish between those who are motivated to use your help and those who are not. This process may very well eliminate 90 percent of the people who ask you for help. Be honest with yourself and others about your need for time to yourself. You must learn to participate and then retreat.

There's no doubt that Dynamic Supportives have the inner resources for transformation. Your strong sense of self will allow you to be introspective in a productive way because you are not afraid to contact the inner self.

Of course, Dynamic Supportives do need quiet time to be in touch with this voice. Meditative approaches can be of benefit to you, but you must have the discipline to make time for such reflection. Then—and this is most important—you must push yourself to put your plans into action. It's a difficult task, but you have to overcome the Dynamic Supportive's tendency to fill notebooks with dreams, interpretations, and wonderful insights— and then let them lie to gather dust. Begin to put these insights to use in your life.

Finally, to avoid the tendency to drift, keep in mind that the time you have is a finite commodity, and the effort you can put forth is limited as well. So take a hard look at how you spend your time and effort, and ask yourself where you can pare down. What sorts of interventions are you best at carrying out? What requests can you refuse? Which people will actually use your help?

With the answers to these questions, you can decide which actions to stick with and which to drop. Don't try to help everyone. Schedule time for your personal renewal—and protect that time.

CREATIVE ASSERTIVES, LIFE'S INTERPRETERS

Some people create when they're encouraged to, some when they're paid to. But when a person creates simply because he or she *has* to, because it's *in* that person to paint, write, act, dance, or make music, and he needs to do so practically as much as he needs to breathe, then that individual is a Creative Assertive.

Creative Assertives are the artists who interpret life for the rest of us, and tell us, through their art, how they see things. (Because asserting one's view of the world, in some medium or another, is what art is all about, Creatives manifest only as Assertives.) The Creative Assertive group is the one that gives color and definition to our experience on this planet and beyond, helping us to perceive implications, nuances, beauty, laughter, and pathos where we might otherwise see only facts—or even nothing. So this group enriches our lives greatly. These are the people who think as much with their hearts as with their minds, and one can't help but admire the quality of their high-end energies. They are thoughtful, giving, gentle, loyal, and idealistic. And they're not afraid to stand up for their ideals, even when that means challenging authority.

Through their art, Creative Assertives continually remind us of what's right and wrong in life. They reflect our social mores, showing us what is beautiful and not so beautiful in society. As philosophers, artists, writers, and the like, they look at society and make a statement about the human condition through their artistic expressions. While some of these expressions receive widespread exposure—examples would be the work of popular filmmakers and authors—some never see the light of day—the poems of a "desk-drawer" poet, for example, or the soliloquies that an unemployed actor can perform only in front of his bathroom mirror. But whatever their level of societal acceptance, people with the creative urge tend to be sensitive and caring. Without these people, the world would be bleak indeed.

Creative Assertives live in a state of high involvement with the environment. They are sensitive to ambient energy and can react emotionally even without knowing exactly what has hit them. As a result, their sense of self can be precarious. Perceptually, they are especially acute and will perceive more than the next person. Where one person sees a tree and a dog, they see a tree and a dog and a hundred other objects and scenes.

Their heightened sensitivity and perceptual ability give them a lot of information to deal with at once, and they sometimes feel they don't know what to make of it all. They absorb a lot from the outside and then reflect back. Sometimes, because they are in a sense conduits for sensation and energy, their feeling for their own identity is weak.

Early on, Creatives must negotiate some potential pitfalls. Given their particular energetic qualities—and society's less-than-understanding reaction to them—they may have childhood experiences that leave them vulnerable as adults. Their energetic and perceptual openness can lead them through a maze of unexpected emotional twists, turns, and flare-ups, and it can make them feel more sensitive than the rest of the world, and inconsistent in the ways in which they cope with life.

The Creative Assertive child may have it even harder if his or her parents and teachers are inconsistent and negative in their mirroring. Parents may feel at a loss to stay attuned to a child whose imaginative life and emotions are so unpredictable and different from their own, and they may find it impossible to experience and mirror joy in the child's efforts.

Thus Creative Assertives tend to be low on joy and to lack confidence in their inner resources. Since their work must stem from creativity, they may continually fear that they will no longer be able to produce or that others will reject them or their work. They often look outside themselves for solutions, self-definition, and guidance. They may throw themselves into someone else's belief systems, for example. These are the people who join New Age cults and other transformational groups by the millions.

Creative Assertives can be so busy searching, analyzing, and seeking themselves in the reactions of others that they miss the opportunity to live in the moment. They spend a lot of time planning for the future or holding on to things that went wrong in the past. In fact, they cling to negative experiences more than any other energy type—and they can exhaust others with an ability to talk about these experiences endlessly. Until they learn, as we all must, to let go and trust the inner self, they can exhaust themselves with constant activity and questions about their essential nature.

The problem is, a person who's always thinking is not necessarily always thinking productively. A Creative Assertive may dwell on issues and questions that do not allow him or her to resolve anything. The same question asked a thousand different ways does not help Creative Assertives become any smarter about themselves. In some cases these superanalytical people must learn to surrender their all-encompassing need to understand life. They have to trust in the process of letting go. They question life more than any other energy type does— and perhaps more than they should.

After all, the real lessons of life are not the ones we are taught; they're the ones we learn through the process of being in the world. Consider the student who asks a Zen master for the answers to a thousand questions so he can be a thousand times smarter. The Zen master says, "I can't answer even one of your questions, and you wouldn't be any smarter if I answered questions for the rest of your life." In essence he is telling the student that we do not understand life through questions and answers. To master life, we must learn to live it. That's the concept Creative Assertives must come to understand.

More than any other energy type, Creative Assertives tend to identify with their persona—that is to say, the identity they consciously fashion for themselves to present to the world. Creatives are the type who wake up in the morning and ask themselves not just "What will I do today?" but also "Who will I be today?" "How will I act?" "How will I seem?" "How do I want others to see me?" They have to plan everything out in terms of the face they will present to the world. It can be a charming face, but at times it's almost as if it's been laboriously pasted on.

Creative Assertives will go out of their way to be helpful and generous to others, wonderful qualities that can work against them if they are overly motivated by a need for acceptance. Creatives swing between intense involvement with others and aloofness—and the latter attitude often predominates at a deep emotional level. They may pretend to themselves that they are powerful, but they are always vulnerable to discovering that they are not strong and perfect. They tend to avoid people and situations that would awaken them from this fantasy.

Male or female, the Creative Assertive has a gentle and sensitive nature. Unlike the Dynamic energies, who would just about bounce back even if you threw them off a cliff, Creative Assertives can break easily. They hurt when they feel unappreciated, and any episode of disrespect or betrayal is like a stab to their heart. Because Creative Assertives are self-sufficient and giving, others may take them for granted or fail to acknowledge their needs. They can be the best of friends and partners, but they must be understood and respected for who they are. They are the roses of life—these creative thinkers and artists—but you would not hold a rose the same way you would a hardier plant.

The Creative Assertive woman can be like Isadora Duncan—not afraid to show the color of her spirit and frequently perceiving herself to transcend physical, emotional, and mental boundaries. She is extremely attractive to men but also quite volatile. As a result, she is the least likely energy type with whom a man will want to have a relationship. Most men like people they can control, and the Creative Assertive woman is uncontrollable because her emotions vacillate so much.

She may become completely immersed in her work for periods of time, and then decide to focus more on relationships because she believes she is missing out on that aspect of life. But she brings the same volatile energy to her relationships that she does to her work. Other people may not be able to handle the intensity of the energy she shares. She can be creative, constructive, vibrant, and joyful, and she has an enormous stretch of mind. But those very qualities will scare off men who want a predictable relationship. A man may be drawn to the energies of a Creative Assertive woman, but her ephemeral quality makes it difficult to find a point of connection. The man goes here, and she's over there. It's an intimidating experience.

Other women are also intimidated by the Creative Assertive woman. She represents the freedom they have not experienced in their own lives. Thus other women will be drawn to the Creative Assertive, but they may not want to form a close friendship with her. Indeed, they may criticize her for being flighty, immature, unstable, or hyperactive. So acquaintances may attend the Creative Assertive woman's performances or invite her to their parties, but they don't necessarily want to live next door to her or invite her to their church or synagogue. After all, she might dress strangely and want to talk about the rabbi in the middle of the service.

The Creative Assertive male also has an unbridled desire to express himself through poetry, writing, art, dance, filmmaking, and the like. He perceives things intensely, with all the definition, nuance, and color that give life its dimensions. Where we see a simple field, for example, he sees an entire landscape and a vast tableau of design. Creative Assertive men, like their female counterparts, are born with a visionary energy that one cannot develop. You either have it or you don't. Those who do can then enhance that energy with education and craftsmanship.

Woody Allen is a Creative Assertive. He's not dynamic or charismatic, but he certainly expresses his view of the world through creative forms. However, he is also an example of how the Creative Assertive's ever-erupting insecurity makes him want to please everyone—that is, as a comic, he became less funny when he started playing to the critics rather than to "plain folks." Interestingly, even Allen himself recognized this dilemma in *Stardust Memories;* in that film one of his characters becomes more involved in pursuing acclaim than in making people laugh.

Unfortunately, the Creative Assertive male is often considered unmasculine. Other men seem to fear that he will threaten their own masculinity. After all, the Creative Assertive male is not likely to subscribe to the stereotypical measures of manliness, such as muscle-flexing or handiness with a football. They express the concept of manhood differently. In fact, they generally are more interested in their role as a human being than in being a "man."

Because the Creative Assertive is not—to put it mildly—society's most highly rewarded type, and because it's often difficult for males, in particular, to manifest their creative sides, many Creative Assertive males in our society are subtly or not so subtly conditioned to be other energy types. Even if a child is not told, "Don't you dare be a poet," he can pick up on the cues. He notices that it's the "artsy" cousin whom family members talk about in somewhat hushed tones, as if he's different, not quite acceptable. Of course, if the cousin becomes extremely successful with his art, the tones may become less hushed, but there's still that taint of going against the normal, all-American grain.

I think of a childhood friend I had who went on to become a small-town football coach with a family and a very normal, responsible kind of life. About ten years ago I went back home to see him, and he said, "Let me show you something."

Now, I'd lived across the street from him, and we'd been the best of buddies practically from the cradle, but what he showed me came as a complete surprise. He pulled out from beneath his bed a big bundle of poems, articles, and book manuscripts he had written. I read them all that day and that night, and I said, "Tom, this is beautiful work! Why are these sitting under your bed?"

He said, "Well, you know, I didn't want anybody to think I was queer and a writer." His conditioning was so strong that he was denying his own creative self. He was living as a conditioned self, as an Adaptive Supportive, and he was not realizing his potential.

I've also seen seeming Dynamic Assertives who are really Creatives at heart. These are people who do everything to be assertive, and yet feel insecure. They're people who should be spending time introspectively creating, but instead they're out there trying to be major honchos because they were told this image was the one for them.

All in all, society seems to be sending mixed messages to Creatives. Most aren't paid well, if at all, for their creative efforts. They're considered a little strange. But we laud a few highly and tolerate the rest, making allowances for their unorthodox behavior because they're artists. They're the ones who reveal the full breadth of our emotional lives, interpreting it and displaying it before us. So we need them.

REACH *IN* AND TOUCH SOMEONE: THE UP AND DOWN SIDES OF CREATIVES

There's an old saying about how easy it is to be a writer—all you have to do is slice open a vein and let everything flow out! This is actually a graphic illustration of how the work of any Creative comes from deep within the person, and while using a razor blade is not the method of choice, accessing one's inner core is always necessary if one is to be a real artist. And herein lies the up-side/down-side dichotomy for Creative Assertives. On the up side, when a Creative is in exquisite touch with his or her innermost reserves of memories and feelings, he can produce great work and be fulfilled doing so. But if a Creative goes one step farther and gets *too much* in touch with his inner memory and feeling bank, he can end up living in the past, rehashing old problems, and forgetting to buy the groceries. This "super-in-touchness" is the down side of the Creative type.

Because they live so much in their minds, Creative Assertives may have trouble making their way in the world. They seek out ideal environments that do not always exist. Other problems: They often swing between extremes in their emotions and levels of activity, and they tend to become narrowly focused on certain aspects of their lives, to the exclusion of equally important areas.

To be healthy, all things must be in balance. One cannot focus strictly on work, relationships, exercise, relaxation, or any other area of life for a long period. Yet all of these things must be tended to, in turn, on a regular basis. On their down side, Creative Assertives may work obsessively and ignore the need to do these other things. When people work excessively, even if they love what they are doing, they deny the other facets of life, to their own detriment. They lose sight of the fact that they're part of a larger world, and they forget how to relax, mellow out, enjoy the company of others, and enjoy life.

When Creative Assertives are on their up side, they will deal with stressors appropriately. But on their down side, they may have an inordinate number of physical ailments because they do not always give themselves time to heal and nurture wellness. They may use illness as a rationale for not achieving their goals or even as a way to gain the attention of others and draw more energy toward themselves. Indeed, some Creatives seem to find in hypochondria a way of gaining needed succor, and being chronically ailing can become a way of life for some.

A sure sign that a Creative Assertive has not developed a strong connection to the inner self is a preoccupation with his or her reputation. Some Creatives need constant reaffirmation that what they've done is good; there can never be enough applause and accolades. Consider the actor who gets depressed if the public is not adoring, or the author who can't take even one bad review. Sometimes, if the Creative Assertive was not mirrored joyfully as a child, he or she becomes afraid to make contact with the inner self for fear there is nothing good—or nothing at all—to discover within. Thus the outside world's reaction to his work becomes the only thing that provides him with a feeling of self-worth.

Part of Creative Assertives' down-side picture is that they can get into power drive, trying to control every aspect of the environment in an effort to banish uncertainty. Their energy is channeled into action and appearances, and they may become flashy and shallow. And if they can't keep up the facade, they often become morose and self-absorbed. Nothing matters but their own pain and problems. They can't see the future.

This moroseness and self-alienation interfere with their ability to create and the quality of their work. When nothing exists except their own world, their art and their connection to others suffer. Soon they spend all their time talking about their problems and pain. They hang on to that pain and ruminate about their limitations and fears. At some point they may try to find themselves at a spiritual or transformational center, but they are generally disappointed with the process because it does not meet their high expectations.

Creative Assertives are always looking for something in life. But they tend to look in the wrong place because they focus on themselves. Rather than look at how they can use life, they look at how they can improve their skills and talents to enhance their creativity. They will take class after class to improve themselves, for example. But in the process they receive false nourishment and avoid the really intractable problems in their lives. It's as if they say, "When I perfect myself, then I'll get into my work, get my work into the world, get into a relationship."

Creative Assertives have a hard time simply being in the world. To enjoy the moment, they would have to let their brains relax. That's tough for them. For instance, if you hand them a rose, they won't simply accept it for what it is. Instead they will analyze the rose, compare it to other roses they have had in the past, and connect it with other events in their lives. The mind never shuts off and they're always someplace else, not in the moment. They are, in fact, the world's biggest worriers. They worry about *everything*. It's probably a result of their highly developed imaginative abilities, but they can imagine all sorts of awful things happening, and sometimes seem to think that keeping these images in their mind will somehow prevent them from actually coming to pass!

Creative Assertives may rationalize their weaknesses into strengths. "I could be in the present, in the body, but I'm too spiritual for that," they may say, or, "I'm not running from the world; I'm just independent." If you ask a Creative Assertive why he or she can't lighten up and enjoy life, a typical response might be that it's impossible to do so in a world filled with suffering. But their seriousness may be taken to extremes and can turn into self-pity.

THE UP-AND-DOWN WORLD OF CREATIVES AT WORK

It isn't easy being a Creative Assertive and working in the real world at the same time. One problem stems from the area of motivation. People are motivated to work by many things—money, prestige, the need to subsist, a feeling of satisfaction. Creative Assertives can be motivated by all of these, but they have another fuel behind their work—the absolute *need* to do whatever they're doing. In other words, a true Creative Assertive *has* to paint, make films, dance, do stand-up comedy, write, sculpt, or whatever. The need is nonnegotiable, really, and sometimes it gets in the way of "normal" functioning.

The complicating factor here is that this need to engage in one's art tends to wax and wane, which means that the Creative Assertive tends to be on a more erratic schedule than the rest of us. Let's say that he's a painter. The nature of the creative urge is such that he may find himself inspired for a period of several days, and feel impelled to paint straight through. At another point he may be all "painted out," and not want to look at a canvas for weeks. The inconstancy of the creative urge can be a problem in terms of taking care of other life responsibilities, which tend to be constant. Creative Assertives, and those they live with, have to keep in mind that you can't regulate artistic output the way you can other types of work. You can try, and obviously there are deadlines that have to be met in any real-world endeavor, but it's going to be difficult at times.

Another problematic aspect of being a creative person, especially if one is making a living from one's art, is that, if it's all coming from within, there always seems to be the chance of everything just drying up, in which case the artist will be completely out of luck. So for Creative Assertives, there's always that worry in the back of their minds that the artistic gift may suddenly and mysteriously desert them, just as mysteriously as it appeared in their lives. Thus the movie star fears that he'll never be invited to do another film; the author, that she'll never publish another book; the painter, that this will be her last painting that's worth anything. The question, "What if the well runs dry?" is a scary one to live with.

Nevertheless, Creatives have to live with this question, and the world has to live with Creatives, because we need them. A lot of what sparkles and shines in our world, and a lot of what inspires people and makes them think, and laugh, and even takes their breath away, is the work of Creative Assertives. The plain fact is that there's no one better for creative work than a Creative Assertive! But in terms of the nitty-gritty of their working conditions, you have to be careful. You have to give them a lot of space to work independently. Otherwise they will burn out and become angry, and they won't want to work with you anymore. I often hire Creative Assertives for short-term projects, for example. To keep the relationship healthy, I give them all the autonomy they want and acknowledge their work. I would never take one of these people and tie them down in an office.

Also, I wouldn't make a Creative Assertive a manager. While members of this energy group are natural doers and creators, you're not likely to find them in positions of authority, because this isn't their forte. Not that they seek out management positions. They generally are not interested in management functions or supervising other people, in part because they are sensitive and do not like to judge others or be judged themselves. They are motivated by the need to create and have their work accepted, not by a desire for money or for control of people or systems.

Creative Assertives aren't necessarily the best choice for ongoing, long-term jobs either, because they tend to be inconsistent. I learned this lesson when I hired a Creative Assertive as a caretaker. He would feel good one week and bad the next; he would milk the cow one week and not the next. This volatility is often part of their nature; after all, if they were consistent, they would also be predictable, which is contrary to the creative energy, in which spurts of enthusiasm and energy contribute to the process.

For ordinary projects that don't require major inspiration, the Creative Assertive works well under pressure. In fact, this group often needs pressure to perform because they tend to procrastinate. Without a deadline, they tend to put off work as long as possible and avoid bringing anything to completion. This problem can be compounded by their perfectionist tendencies. They will continually rework a product because they are never satisfied with the results. At some point others simply have to tell them, "Time's up!"

Creative Assertives tend to measure their self-worth with everything they do, a propensity that can be both positive and destructive. If they don't like something they've created, or if they do not succeed with a project, they take it personally. Any barriers they encounter will be taken personally as well. It's as if the barrier were made exclusively for them, and they can become very frustrated and overly focused on the barrier itself.

In short, the world of work can be a roller coaster for Creative Assertives. They're intermittently motivated. In a good mood, they're productive dynamos; in a bad mood, they become despondent. They accelerate as they get involved in their work, then gradually decline into apathy. The continuity found in other energy types, and in most of life, may be lacking in the Creative Assertive. They have trouble determining if their creative ebb and flow result from psychological blocking or a natural process. So they fret and analyze some more.

RELATIONSHIPS—CYCLIC, COMPLEX

When it comes to getting close to others, Creative Assertives can be skittish if they have not yet learned to appreciate themselves. They will be alternately intense and distant; they approach and avoid. They can drain another person of energy with their need for mirroring and appreciation, then retreat into an aestheticized aloofness.

Creative Assertives also tend to idealize a few special people and populate their lives with nonequals. They may seek out people with strong personalities who they imagine can guide them through life, or people who can enhance their self-esteem. Thus they may end up with few true friends who will challenge and support them in a constructive and realistic way. Until the Creative Assertive learns to actualize his or her creative gifts in the world, he or she will squander energy in fantasy accomplishments and relationships.

Creative Assertives generally know a lot of people, but they may not have a lot of friends or lasting relationships. Even so, Creatives leave a legacy with those who have known them. Others may have a hard time bonding with a Creative Assertive because they can't move fast enough to meet his or her many expectations, but they will undoubtedly remember something about the person. They'll remember his or her creativity, vitality, or unusual view of the world; however, they may not remember the Creative Assertive as someone they wanted in their life, because the relationship was so draining.

Indeed, Creative Assertives often have intense and volatile relationships. They will bend over backwards to be supportive and encouraging, but once they are comfortable in a relationship, their energy may change if they dwell on problems from the past. They may spend a lot of time focusing on their problems—and relating them to a partner or friend over and over again—because they don't know how to resolve conflicts. They don't know how to let go and move forward. Creative Assertives ask questions that do not need a resolution. They lay a hand where there is no need to be touched. It's as if they finish a recipe and then start all over again. They have a difficult time letting things be.

Creative Assertives also tend to find faults in everyone, including themselves, their friends, and their partners. When that happens, it doesn't mean they don't love you, and it's not a sign of rejection. They simply cannot accept things as they are, and must analyze everything and everyone around them. But they will never be as tough on others as they are on themselves. Creative Assertives are tougher on themselves than are any other energy types. They continually challenge and punish themselves. But they are the only energy type that will use self-criticism as an avenue for change.

Their sensitivity can make them quite defensive. Therefore, others who interact with Creative Assertives must be constantly aware of the little emotional minefields they have planted all around them. If a partner or friend triggers one of these minefields—for example, by asking about their work, their motives for doing certain types of work, their inability to let go of pain—the Creative Assertive may very well respond with an emotional explosion. And if asked to sweep away these defensive minefields, the Creative Assertive may not be able to do so.

On their down side, Creative Assertives have a fear of failure. Their self-esteem can be badly damaged if they fail at an endeavor or do not succeed to the degree they anticipated. Their inability to bounce back from a failure can affect other aspects of their life. Real, perceived, or anticipated failure can leave them stuck in a rut. Then their fear of being hurt by others only complicates the picture, and with these two fears at work, the openness a Creative Assertive brings to his or her art may be lacking on a personal, human level. Underneath the charming exterior, the Creative Assertive has taken cover in emotional distance. What you get is the persona.

Consequently, the relationship can be boring because on the Creative Assertive's end it does not come from the self. His or her emotions do not come from the moment. The relationship may become unnecessarily heavy and intense, and eventually one or the other can't take it anymore. Once they separate, Creative Assertives generally will distrust relationships for a while. They throw themselves back into their work. Eventually they may reenter a relationship and start the cycle again.

Relating with Creative Assertives requires patience, because their needs are not simple, and they change. Members of this group appear to be quite independent, but it's more complicated than that. They need time alone to focus on their creative spirit. And while they need others periodically, they also may fear they will be overwhelmed by the strong personalities to whom they often gravitate. They want to be admired, but their fear of failure may send them off into their corners, where they can hide their imperfections.

While Creative Assertives are indeed giving, supportive, and cooperative people, they may have a tendency to do things for others simply to be recognized and to enhance their self-esteem. They will help another person in any way possible, thereby showing that they are giving; in return, they expect that person to acknowledge their efforts. If he or she does not, the Creative Assertive will be hurt by the experience and withdraw.

Many people hesitate to get close to a Creative Assertive because they have a tough time handling their periodic need for space, and their volatility. If you were to come across a log, for example, you probably wouldn't do anything to change it. You would simply sit on the log and let it be. The Creative Assertive, on the other hand, might decide to dance on the log or to paint a picture of it; he or she might write a poem about it or even whittle a carving out of it. The point is that you never know what they will do, which can be disconcerting.

Creative Assertive men may have a difficult time with women. Not only are relationships of secondary importance to them, but they also have an intense need, at times, to be alone to create. During this phase they may work twenty hours a day, seven days a week, for months on end. Think of Hemingway, Faulkner, Joyce, Picasso, or Renoir. They put this type of intensity into their work, while neglecting other aspects of their lives, because they were fueled by passion.

At some point, though, the Creative Assertive man will shift to the other extreme and experience an intense loneliness and need to bond. He'll want to mellow out and balance his life, but he may burn out the woman in his life because he puts the same energy into the relationship that he puts into his work. He wants the relationship too much, and his emotions are volatile. His tendency to swing between the two extremes of intense work and intense relationship, never staying at either end for very long, does not make him that desirable a partner, at least to those with more conventional expectations.

Female Creative Assertives are similar. They generally have one-on-one friendships. They may appear shy and hesitant at first, but will eventually come to trust someone once they are comfortable with the relationship. But they, too, may swing between being distant and involved in their own energy and being too closely involved with the other person's energy.

Creative Assertives are reluctant joiners, which affects their ability to develop relationships. They're often secretive and reclusive. And they may not be able to connect with others because their ideas are unique and difficult to share with people who are not of similar mind. Consequently they may feel most comfortable with others who share the same energy and can appreciate their lifestyle and way of thinking. While another creative person may be involved in a totally different field, at least he or she understands what it is to create and to be alone in the process.

Family life is problematic for Creative Assertives. Their intense need for emotional support surfaces in the safety of the family, which they tend to use and to blame. They may not make ideal parents or relatives for that reason. They can be particularly difficult parents if they have not learned to contain their emotional highs and lows, confusion, and neediness. They can be easily distracted by their search for meaning in life, and they may not give quality time and attention to the people around them, including their children. While it's not their nature to intentionally hurt another person, unintentional neglect can create uncertainty in the family setting.

Energy Combinations

On their up side, Creative Assertives are capable of quiet, harmonious relationships. If they pair with someone who has the same energy or a complementary one, they can be content and productive. But they can have tortured relationships as well if they end up with the wrong partner. And even if they are miserable, they may stick with it and feel martyred.

An energy pair with promise is that of the Creative Assertive and the Dynamic Assertive, who can make a beautiful combination, especially when they are both on their up side. They can have a wonderful, trusting relationship and a dynamic exchange of ideas. For example, they may both work for common causes that broaden the perspective of other people's lives and enhance the quality of their own.

One has the vision; the other has the creative skills. Bring these two qualities together and you have the big picture and the ability to carry it out. The Dynamic Assertive can identify an important issue and bring it to the public's attention, while the Creative Assertive can produce the campaign—the posters, documentaries, or movie scripts—that brings the issue to life and promotes change. It's one of the best combinations you can have. All Dynamic Assertives, in fact, should work with a Creative Assertive to see a project to completion. They are not only patient, but also supportive, cooperative, and loyal. They're sensitive, and they truly care about others.

However, a Creative Assertive may be drawn to a Dynamic Assertive for the wrong reasons. For example, if a Creative Assertive woman has not yet found fulfillment through her art, she may identify with the creative quality of the Dynamic Assertive and form a relationship with that person because she wants to discover his "formula." She assumes the Dynamic Assertive is fulfilled, and she wants to find out how he's doing it. But the Dynamic Assertive may be moving forward at such a rapid speed that the Creative Assertive, who is usually more past-oriented, feels overwhelmed and frustrated.

Two Creative Assertives could have a wonderful relationship if both are on the high end and are manifesting their creativity. The results won't be the same as with the Dynamic Assertive/Creative Assertive combination, because a Creative Assertive does not involve other people the way a Dynamic Assertive does. But the relationship can be beautiful because each respects the other's expression of life through art. Both will tend to be trusting, giving, and sympathetic, and the relationship will be fulfilling as long as they can deal with their problems. The newness that automatically springs from the mind of a Creative Assertive will be injected into the relationship. One caveat about a Creative/Creative pair: If they're both in the exact same field, the inevitable competition could be a big problem. The relationship has a much better chance of survival if the two are in related or divergent artistic fields.

A Creative Assertive can have a good relationship with a Dynamic Supportive, and with an Adaptive Supportive as well. Both can provide the unconditional love and support the Creative Assertive needs. A possible problem is that the Creative Assertive's tendency to fret and complain will eventually wear on the Adaptive Supportive, who is likely to be a more relaxed and calm person.

THE CHALLENGE: LET GO OF THE PAST

Creative Assertives are drawn to peak experiences. They go out and search for these experiences through their creativity, performances, and dialogue with other people. However, because they look for these experiences "out there," rather than within themselves, they don't always find them.

A down-side tendency evident in many artists is that they look inward for artistic material but not for ways to grow spiritually. So they live with old pain. Yes, they make feeble attempts to escape the pain, but since these are not vigorous enough, it's like trying to get out of quicksand by moving up and down rather than moving forward. They're stuck in the quicksand, and their relationships may be stuck as well.

Creatives tend to thrive on their bad experiences, which can keep them locked and prevent them from making changes in their lives. They will try to achieve change by taking one step forward. They'll grab on to every guru, ashram, book, and New Age process they can find. The problem is, one foot is still planted. Despite all the motion, they haven't really changed. They *could* change. Creative Assertives certainly have the intellect to do so. But, strangely, it's often as if they have learned the lessons of the desert so well that they avoid the oasis just ahead.

Transformation comes only when the body, mind, and belief system change, when one truly gives up the past. By relinquishing the past, Creative Assertives can free themselves to be in the moment. Then their responses, attitudes, beliefs, and values can be created in the present. If I was a racist yesterday, it doesn't mean I have to be a racist today. If I didn't exercise yesterday, it doesn't mean I can't exercise today.

The power of any person—not just Creatives—resides only in the present; that is, a person can only do things *now*; no one on earth can do things yesterday. But when people surrender the power they possess to remembrances from the past, then their pain, guilt, fears, and insecurity will dictate the moment. They won't be comfortable with the here and now; they'll be in the past and, no doubt, resenting the fact that they are.

What's missing for many Creative Assertives is a forward momentum. It's frustrating to take a step ahead but never really get anywhere. They've got all this motion going, but they're really not moving forward. Creative Assertives spend a lot of time trying to figure out why this is so—why they are not moving forward, why they are not more dynamic, why they cannot enjoy life more. They can become like the Woody Allen character in movies—the type who's had his problems analyzed for so many years that he's the world's most highly educated neurotic. But he's still got the problems because he hasn't let go of them. Woody Allen manages to make this situation seem hilarious on screen, but for Creative Assertives stuck in this rut, it's not really funny.

What Creative Assertives don't realize is that the answers generally lie with their failure to disconnect from the past and to believe in their own efficacy. They are limited by their attachment to guilt, previous experiences, and supposed rights. The irony is that Creative Assertives aspire not to have limits, but in many cases they are held back by self-imposed limits.

Creative Assertives have trouble trusting in themselves, unless they are at the high end. They will question their previous values—and analyze them ad nauseam—but they will not change those values. It's the same barrier they face again and again in life—a fear of truly looking inward.

The process of growth for Creative Assertives is complicated by their inability to deal with confusion. If something confuses them, it stops them cold. They have to spend time analyzing it. And it's usually an issue in their own life that confuses them, such as the nature of their relationships, the nature of their work, the reasons for their work, the reality of their life, the reasons people either accept or reject them. These questions stem, in part, from the sense of personal unreality that can permeate their lives. They conjure up position statements to replace the answers that would come from listening for guidance from within. They're afraid that nothing will come if they let their intuition take over, and they can't bear the anxiety of anticipation.

What's more, the disappointments of life often cause depression in Creative Assertives, more so than in any other energy type. They generally lack the emotional wherewithal to overcome disappointments, so they stop themselves from progressing. They put their life and their energy on hold, even as they go through the motions of living.

GO WITH THE FLOW—AND THE EBB

If you're a Creative Assertive, you've probably known it for a long time. But you may not have known that the idea of the "tortured artist" is not something that has to apply to you. The key is understanding yourself, and understanding and managing the creative process you engage in.

First, you have to learn to tolerate your creative ebbs and flows, so you don't interpret them as signs of personal strength or failure.

The ebb and flow of creativity are natural parts of your being. It's like a natural circadian rhythm, with low energy, high energy, and low energy again, although the cycle may last much longer than a day; it could extend over a week, a month, or more, and contain mini-cycles within it. The point to remember is that if you try to sustain the high energy at all times, you may fall prey to artificial stimulants such as drugs. You'll burn out as you try to force a creative mood beyond its natural limits. Likewise, you need to move beyond the low energy and pull yourself out of depression—not necessarily by resuming the creative process, but by doing other things for a while. You'll probably only feed the depression if you think you have to be heavily involved in creativity at all times, because you'll be disappointed to discover that this is impossible.

It might help to think of your creative force as a pendulum. Rather than going up and down, it swings from left to right—from a period of creativity to one of rest and renewal. Think of the latency period as a seasonal change; the tree is not always in bloom. You can't be creative every day. You need time to reflect and engage in life, just as a dedicated athlete must have time to rest and rebalance between competitive events. Indeed, many of our great artists have gone out into the world, experienced life, and then returned to interpret it through their art. So go out and experience life, then come back and interpret it. After all, you may have nothing to express if you do not engage in life yourself.

An important task for Creative Assertives is to develop a real sense of self. This is a difficult task if their self-esteem has taken a beating over the years. Their particular energy makes them feel self-inconsistent. As a result, they look outward to find out what others want them to do and be. They don't know who they are, and they spend too much time immersed in fantasies about being special. They don't deserve the same hardships as other people, they think. There must be some mistake. I'll just go find that nice creative high, and that way I won't have to think about these problems anymore. In this way they tend to run from the person or situation that will drag them back to earth.

As a Creative Assertive you must learn to appreciate yourself. Find the courage to be truthful about who you are, develop a set of values, and then put them to work. Otherwise you will never be able to bring your work into the world and you will feel too much pressure in relationships. You will spend your time coming and going, embracing and fleeing.

The goal for the Creative Assertive is self-discovery, under the guidance of the inner self. Inner-directedness must be developed, and the imagination must be gotten under control. If not, all your energy will be dissipated by feel-better fantasies, and the imagination will remain superficial. Stop running around and start listening to yourself. Don't waste your energy envying others and looking for praise. Stop doing things to make yourself liked by others. The accolades you seek must come from your own ego admiring your own self.

Once you create a relationship with your inner self and find your creative drive, you can take it out into the world. Many Creative Assertives get stuck in the first stage and remain forever in a state of dreamy self-absorption. Your work has to pass from thought to form.

Learn to recognize what's going on in your creative life. If you feel restless and unproductive, but still enthusiastic about what you're doing or plan to do, don't worry. Small blocks such as these are part of the creative process. Conversely, if you feel as if you don't care, that nothing's happening, you need to work on yourself. But don't run off to take a course or buy another book. Don't start questioning yourself, asking if you're really talented, and don't make excuses for not working. Instead, learn to experience the moment. It will invigorate you. Try to manifest your thoughts in your work; if you fail, try again.

If you're like the typical Creative, you also have to let go of yesterday. Loosen your mutual stranglehold with the past. It's not that you have to reject the past completely, but you have to take a step away from it. Use your memories for your work, but then step away from them so you can really relate to the person you are with at the moment. In that way you'll be giving the person you are with—and that includes your present self, too!—a fair shake.

A final challenge for the Creative Assertive: You have to learn to manage your special energetic openness and perceptual acuity. You have to shut down your perceptual venetian blinds, as it were, withdraw, and take time for yourself. Thus you can renew your spirit as you prepare to enjoy your creativity once again.

MOST OF THE PEOPLE YOU'LL EVER MEET: ADAPTIVE SUPPORTIVES

The various Dynamics and the Creatives, interesting though they are, actually comprise only a small segment of the population. Let's look now at the natural life energy group that includes most of the people you'll ever meet—about 90 percent, in fact. This NLE group's numbers, and the volume and type of work it gets done, make it arguably the most important one of all. What is this single largest energy category in our society? It's the Adaptive Supportives. And in a lot of ways, when we talk about "our society" or "our culture," it's the Adaptive Supportives we're referring to. Because there are so many of them, their values and way of life pervade our culture, and this is true not just of the United States, but universally.

Adaptive Supportives have many positive qualities— as a rule they are loyal, giving, and easygoing in their approach to life. What's more, they can be very hard

135

workers and highly conscientious about their work, both in terms of doing a good job and providing for their families. And since these are the people who tend to work at society's more menial and physically demanding jobs, sticking with a job year after year sometimes constitutes an unrecognized act of heroism on the part of members of this group. After all, working fifty hours a week managing a corporate department or writing novels might, in certain respects, be considered hard, but working fifty hours a week cleaning people's houses or putting together cars on an assembly line is *hard work.*

Despite hardships, this is a group that knows how to grasp opportunities for happiness. They do so in the best, most realistic way—by enjoying the small, common pleasures of life. So a family picnic, going to the drive-in movies, going to a shopping mall on a Saturday, receiving a Christmas card, sending a Christmas card, participating in a charity bake sale—all these things can bring a lot of joy to an Adaptive Supportive.

And note this well: Being able to extract joy from everyday things is a gift not everyone has. Not to denigrate the energy groups we've looked at so far, but consider how some of them would approach a family picnic. A Creative Assertive might not want to go because she'd be mentally rehashing a fight she had with another family member half a decade ago, so the picnic would be too traumatic. A Dynamic Aggressive wouldn't be able to go because her appointment book would be completely filled for the next year. Besides, there wouldn't be enough important people at the picnic; you can't network with toddlers and elderly aunts. A Dynamic Assertive might actually show up, but end up haranguing everyone for bringing along a portable

TV, or for using too many Styrofoam cups and despoiling the environment. An Adaptive Supportive, on the other hand, would actually enjoy the whole event—the anticipatory fun of the preparation, the picnic meal itself—complete with demanding toddlers and the football game on in the background, the camaraderie of the cleanup.

Again, the joys of this group are not grandiose; they don't involve elaborate schemes. They're little, subtle things. And this is all part of the picture of Adaptive Supportives at their best; when they're on their up side, there's a genteelness to these people, there's an order to their lives and a functional balance to them that make everything seem as if it's exactly the way it should be.

THE MALLEABLE MAINSTREAM

In another area, though, this group has a problematic aspect that can't be ignored. In fact, the history of the world rides on this aspect, and it always has—sometimes in the wrong direction. The problem is that this group can be manipulated by authority figures. Adaptive Supportives are the followers in life—the vast majority of the people who adapt their lives to prevailing belief systems and live a narrowly defined existence. Rarely do they challenge those in power, no matter how wrong their belief systems may appear to be.

The irony is that Adaptive Supportives could be a tremendous force in society, simply by virtue of their numbers. But most Adaptive Supportives fail to recognize the power of the individual in effecting constructive change, and instead seek the security of anonymity. By conforming to the expectations of the majority, they relieve themselves of responsibility for their own lives. Of course, this approach to living is a trade-off, requiring them to give away their power to others. If Adaptive Supportives were to recognize their power and band together as a collective force, they would, like a tidal wave, wash over the people who control them.

Unfortunately, that scenario is rarely a threat to the people in power. Adaptive Supportives are motivated, in large part, by a need to be accepted by others. Their whole lifestyle is supportive of the status quo, and they thrive on the sense of belonging that comes from "fitting in." But to do so, they must deny their individuality and independent thought. Once they take this route in life, which they're conditioned to do from childhood on, they become dependent on the approval of others. Adaptive Supportives need to know that they are part of a larger group, and they derive their identity from their relationship to the majority.

They generally have a fixed notion of what is right or wrong, and so, throughout life, Adaptive Supportives resist any challenge to their belief systems from the nonconformists in society. They don't like to change, and they certainly don't want to accept anything that is new or different. Adaptive Supportives conform to group standards in all situations—their homes, workplaces, places of religion, and so forth. By doing so, they get the reinforcement they need from others and buttress their sense of belonging. They make a statement that they are like the others with whom they are aligned.

But the desire to be like others exposes us to some pitfalls. For one, we lose our sense of the uniqueness of individuals. By creating a collective concept of themselves and submerging their identity in that of the group, Adaptive Supportives deny the qualities that make individuals different. They suppress their own individuality, and they expect others to suppress theirs for the sake of the group. That philosophy can lead to some perverse cultures. Consider Japan, where the concept of "I" has little meaning. The needs of the company take precedence over the needs of the individual. As a result, independent thought is discouraged and the masses become obedient and intolerant.

The real danger with Adaptive Supportives is that they will cling to faulty belief systems. They have a strong need to trust in one authority, and they feel vulnerable and threatened if an idea or person challenges that authority. When Adaptive Supportives are presented with alternatives to an established paradigm—in politics, religion, or even something as practical as approaches to health care—they have a difficult time rejecting their original belief and shifting to another. In essence they don't want to hear both sides of an argument, they don't want to consider an opposing viewpoint, and they don't want to change how they think and feel.

The crux of the matter is this: The process of change threatens Adaptive Supportives' sense of security, which is of utmost importance to them. They place great value in feeling secure—in their homes, jobs, and relationships. This is the group that often stays for decades with jobs that offer a steady paycheck, regardless of whether the work is satisfying or even threatens their health. They tend to stay in bad marriages as long as these make them feel secure. They remain obedient to authority figures who acknowledge and meet their need for security. Adaptive Supportives pride themselves on permanency; they derive comfort from knowing in advance exactly how their lives will be played out.

But when security becomes paramount, the chances are good that other vital issues will not be addressed. In fact, Adaptive Supportives may ignore such issues when they pose a threat to their sense of security. If you work in a corrupt government agency, will you challenge that corruption and jeopardize your job security? If you work in a company that pollutes the environment, will you question its policies and put a regular paycheck at risk? For most Adaptive Supportives, the answer to such troubling questions is no. They choose to support that which keeps them secure.

It's not surprising, then, that Adaptive Supportives often live with a feeling of powerlessness. They relinquish control over their own lives, giving more power to authority figures than they do to themselves. This gives them a myopic view of life and closes off many avenues of growth and transformation. For example, Adaptive Supportives rarely challenge doctors on the treatments they prescribe, no matter how questionable those treatments may be. If you were to provide Adaptive Supportives with evidence that a particular type of surgery does not correct the problem it supposedly helps—and that, in fact, it harms many of the people who undergo it—most would still have the operation themselves if the doctor told them to.

The tendency of Adaptive Supportives not to question authority goes hand in hand with their having structured their lives within narrow confines. They let society define the parameters of their existence, and as long as they stay within the socially prescribed notions of what is right and wrong, they feel happy and safe. The problem is that their belief systems can become a kind of false mini-reality, an intellectual island of sorts that contains everything they consider necessary for survival. Paradise could be a hundred feet away, but Adaptive Supportives will stick with what they have been conditioned to accept. And if that particular reality causes them pain—in a relationship or job, for example—they do what they must to adapt and survive. They resist change even when the current situation creates discomfort or pain.

It's not that Adaptive Supportives don't recognize an injustice or feel angry about it. They are intelligent and giving people who most certainly empathize with the pain of others. But they tend to hitch their social consciousness to that of a Dynamic Assertive spokesperson, and if none is available, they won't act. Theoretically, no one should need a leader to stand up to an injustice and demand change. But Adaptive Supportives do. So they will adapt to negative forces they encounter, be it pollution in their water or toxic dumps in their backyards, until a Dynamic leader or leaders show them that protest and change are possible. Sometimes they have to be shown again and again before they will act. In addition, it helps if many other Adaptive Supportives are getting on the bandwagon at the same time. Members of this group are joiners by nature, and the safety that seems to come with numbers appeals to them.

Sometimes Adaptive Supportives may seem blind to the possibilities of protest and change, but it's not usually as simple as that. It's an anxiety issue. These people may know intellectually that something in society needs to be corrected, but they don't want to stick their necks out to get the job done. They're caught between what they know should be done and what they are fearful of doing. They're comfortable enough where they are; and even if they're not, they fear that change will cause even more discomfort. "Why risk it?" they think. "I'll just make do with what I have."

The reality, of course, is that life is changing all around them anyway. The world doesn't stand still because we deny the need for change. But Adaptive Supportives may let others do the hard work of change for them. In East Germany, all it took were about seventy-five thousand people to bring the government down. Where were the tens of millions of other people who stood to benefit from democracy? Why weren't they protesting in the streets, helping to bring about the process of change? There weren't because they were not of a change-oriented life energy.

When Adaptive Supportives do change, it's usually because an authority figure has given them "permission" to do so. When the authority in their lives changes, they'll shift course and go along with whatever the leader expects of them. If the pope were to allow women to become priests, the masses would adapt to the change and support it. If the president of the United States were to become a vegetarian, tens of millions of Americans would follow suit and become vegetarians as well. Unfortunately, this approach to change is not the best, since authority, and not independent thought, is still the driving force.

Adaptive Supportives consider themselves to be an extension of authority—and they operate from the assumption that since the authority figure is always right, they, too, are right. This attitude not only causes them to avoid change but also makes them highly obedient. They entrust so much power to authority figures that they may fail to challenge the most obvious wrongs committed by those figures. Throughout the Vietnam War, there was never a demonstration of more than three hundred thousand. The Adaptive Supportives did not show up, even though they, ironically, were the very people that the authorities sent off to do the fighting.

The inescapable fact is that Adaptive Supportives can be easily manipulated, given their obedient nature. They'll obey to the extent of killing people—even to the extent of killing total innocents and children—and even killing themselves—if an authority figure tells them to do so. After all, it wasn't mainly the higher-ups who killed more than six million Jews and many additional millions of others during World War II. And think about this: Thousands of Iranian children died on one summer day when their mothers sent them walking across a minefield. The reason? The Iranian army didn't want its tanks to be destroyed, so someone had to go across first. The mothers gave their children little prayer books and sent them off to die. They did what was "right" according to their religious beliefs and their doctrine of obedience to the law. They were "just following orders."

Granted, episodes such as these are extreme. But they do point out the dangers of the collective mentality. In everyday life this mindset can slowly wear away at Adaptive Supportives. By following the dictates of others—by doing what is asked of them—Adaptive Supportives eventually come to mistrust themselves. Their conditioned beliefs become all-important, and they deny the real self. They become disengaged from life and detached from their true feelings and thoughts. The ultimate outcome is that they may deny responsibility for themselves—for their physical, intellectual, emotional, and spiritual health.

FROM HEROISM TO HEDONISM: THE UP AND DOWN SIDES OF ADAPTIVE SUPPORTIVES

When Adaptive Supportives operate from the high side of their energy, they have many positive qualities. Foremost among them is their giving nature. These are the people who give to charities, answer phones at telethons, and volunteer their time to all sorts of worthy organizations. On their up side they recognize human suffering and do what they can to help others. Adaptive Supportives can be extraordinarily generous in all the small ways that have meaning—cooking food for a fund-raiser, for example, or sharing what they have with a neighbor in need. They can be a great force for good when they are properly guided.

They also have, as we've mentioned, a wonderful ability to appreciate the subtle joys in life. Adaptive Supportives don't need cruises to exotic ports or visits to pricey restaurants in order to experience pleasure. They can find joy in the seemingly small experiences, such as that family picnic we discussed, or a class play, or an evening of bowling. Their capacity to recognize the simple joys in life suggests a sensitivity that everyone should strive to achieve, and the other energy types

144

could take a lesson from Adaptive Supportives in this area.

Adaptive Supportives possess what you might call a soft energy—that is, there is a delicate quality to their interactions with others. They often have a quiet attitude and a natural shyness. In fact, one of their finest qualities is humility—a characteristic that is sorely lacking in some energy types. Adaptive Supportives can be humble, sincere, and trusting. They also have an easygoing approach to life, a lightness of attitude that makes them pleasant to be around. They have a nice sense of humor, and can be playful. Nevertheless, when push comes to shove, this is one tough group of people who know how to activate their survival skills. For instance, in recent years, as job opportunities have disappeared in the eastern industrial states, many Adaptive Supportives have migrated with their families to the Sunbelt to seek new employment. It takes gumption to pick up and move to a new region, especially when there's no guarantee that things will work out there.

Adaptive Supportives' sense of loyalty is another fine quality, provided they are able to withdraw their allegiance from someone or some entity that no longer deserves it. (The phrase "My country, right or wrong" comes to mind here. Supporting one's country when it's right is one thing; however, considering the history of the twentieth century, loyalty to one's country when it's perpetrating wrongful deeds is a morally bankrupt concept whose time has gone.) But on the positive side, Adaptive Supportives are unsurpassed in their capacity to be extremely loyal to a friend or mate. The part of the traditional marriage vow that refers to the partners remaining faithful to each other whether they're richer or poorer, in sickness or in health, is not just a bunch of empty, flowery words for many an Adaptive Supportive. They mean what they say with this vow, and many provide shining examples of dedication both to the ideal of marriage and to their own spouses.

Adaptive Supportives can have tremendous courage as well, especially when they are acting according to the higher ideals of their belief systems. They will sacrifice their lives for the values in which they believe. Adaptive Supportives are the first to charge into battle to fight an enemy or support their homeland in a just cause. They're the first to rush into a burning building to save the life of another human being. When they use their courage properly, Adaptive Supportives are to be admired greatly.

On the low end of the energy spectrum, the Adaptive Supportive is another person entirely. They close down inside, shutting themselves off from the world around them. They lose their vital connection to the issues that have meaning for themselves and others. In this phase, many Adaptive Supportives are completely oblivious to their environment. They will sit by idly as their water, air, and soil are polluted with toxins—and do absolutely nothing about it. They don't speak out against the polluters themselves, and they don't even lend their support to others who attempt to bring about positive change.

Another down-side tendency of Adaptive Supportives is that they do not consider issues in depth. Their goal is to avoid potential conflict, so they hunker down in the security of their homes, their jobs, their day-to-day routines. All of their respect and loyalty are channeled to one authority, and any new idea that challenges that authority only confuses them. So Adaptive Support-ives will position themselves on one side of an issue, then stay there no matter what kind of evidence or logi-cal exposition proves them wrong. And if fear is thrown into the mix, then logic has no chance whatsoever with most Adaptive Supportives. That's why the really shrewd demagogue always peppers his rhetoric with a good amount of fear-mongering. There may be nothing to be afraid of, but he'll make something up just to keep the Adaptive Supportives in line.

At their worst, Adaptive Supportives will do what-ever an authority figure tells them to do. They operate from an unthinking, unfeeling sense of obedience that allows them to take part in highly destructive acts. Adaptive Supportives will carry out the orders of others without ever considering the morality of what they are doing. As long as the person in control acknowledges their need for security, they will remain obedient. What's more, they can degenerate into a mob mentality; Adaptive Supportives are the ones who will boo a per-former off the stage or throw beer cans at a baseball player.

Adaptive Supportives tend to have more health prob-lems than any other energy type. On their high end, they will take some steps to improve their health, such as eating organic produce, taking vitamins, or exercising. More often, however, their diet is terrible—full of junk food, chemical-laden refined foods, and fat. When their health suffers as a result, they often use illness as an excuse not to participate in life. Their sickness becomes a crutch, and they refuse to make constructive changes in their diet and lifestyle.

Many serious disorders and diseases—such as arthritis, heart disease, and cancer—seem to be especially prevalent among Adaptive Supportives. This phenomenon stems, in part, from their tendency to repress their thoughts and feelings, to avoid resolving the conflicts in their lives, and to toe the line by remaining obedient to authority. The connection here is that obedience is often accompanied by a silent rage, and repressed anger has been shown to have deleterious physical consequences.

In fact, Adaptive Supportives are masters of sublimation on their down side. They go for every kind of escapism society has to offer—television, spectator sports, junk food, alcohol, drugs, and supermarket tabloids. Adaptive Supportives are the armchair quarterbacks who overidentify with a sports team, reliving all the intricacies of a game for days afterward and living vicariously through the athletes' victories, defeats, and—perhaps most important—their exciting risk-taking, which is part of each game, but not usually part of an Adaptive Supportive's day. They are the people who see Clint Eastwood movies so they can identify with the force of good against evil. These diversions give them a momentary reprieve from the predictability and boredom of their lives.

More damaging, however, is the Adaptive Supportive's use of addictive products to quell the pain he or she feels—the pain of a bad relationship, the pain of doing unsatisfying work, the pain of not being appreciated by others. Rather than identify the source of the problem, resolve the issue, and move forward with their lives, many Adaptive Supportives suppress the pain by escaping into addictions. They distract themselves from any potential conflict in their lives with caffeine, alcohol, cigarettes, cocaine, tranquilizers, and other medications.

These addictions often stem from their sense of powerlessness. On the down side Adaptive Supportives feel a loss of control over their own lives. But rather than take steps to regain control, they become anxious, cynical, and despondent. That's when they turn to products such as alcohol to take their minds off the problem at hand. The Japanese offer a classic example of this. Because their society does not recognize the importance of the individual, many Japanese "company men" spend their evenings in a state of intoxication. Getting drunk allows them to escape the stringent expectations of society and to release some of their natural energy. Drunk, they can act as they wish, rather than as society tells them they must.

RELATIONSHIPS—STRONG BONDS, EVEN LIFELONG ROMANCE

The single most important element in an Adaptive Supportive's life is often family relationships; everything else in life revolves around these. This group tends to establish secure, long-lasting, and monogamous relationships. They take their emotional bonds seriously and value the stability of their home lives.

It's not unusual for Adaptive Supportives to marry at a young age, even in their teens, and to stay married for the rest of their lives. In many cases, they marry young because they want to wake up in the morning and know they have the love and support of their mate. That assurance in life has more meaning to them than any momentary thrill they might get from a more exotic life-

149

style. Adaptive Supportives want stability, and they are willing to forgo some of life's adventures to attain it. But many marry young for another reason as well. They lack the aspirations that drive dynamic energies, and thus they escape into marriage and the family unit at an early age. Rarely do they strike out on their own in an exploration of life.

Nonetheless, Adaptive Supportives have some fine qualities to contribute to a relationship. They are easygoing and sensitive people who will open themselves up to others. It's as if they are waiting to be experienced by another person and willing to be explored. They are capable of living in the moment and enjoying it, so they can be very sensual. What's more, there's no harshness or aggressiveness to their natural energy when it comes to forming relationships. Adaptive Supportives are willing to give a partner love and respect, and they want to receive the same in return.

In addition, Adaptive Supportives are utterly loyal to their partners—a positive quality that generally serves them well in life. Of course, this same characteristic can lead a person to stay in a bad relationship and end up with a lifetime of heartache. So Adaptive Supportives have to be careful, or they can become trapped in a relationship with an abusive mate. Their sense of obligation—and overwhelming need for security—can keep them in some awful situations.

Another potential problem for Adaptive Supportives is that their partners may attempt to change their natural energy. Some people have a hard time accepting Adaptive Supportives as they are. For example, an Adaptive Supportive's partner may consider his or her shyness to be a personality flaw, and then try to "correct" it by drawing him or her out. These people don't recognize that an Adaptive Supportive's energy can serve as a moderating force in the relationship. In addition, a person's true energy should be respected, not fought.

Adaptive Supportives who find the right partner often form highly symbiotic relationships. Their relationships become truly equal in that each person's needs are fulfilled and each is contributing all he or she can to the good of the marriage. If one partner is working outside the home and one is working within it, this doesn't matter; the important thing is that both are contributing in the best ways they can to the relationship.

Sometimes you'll see a couple who are both Adaptive Supportives who have a relationship that lasts a lifetime, and yet they don't seem to communicate. Other people may not understand how this can be—how, they ask themselves, can a couple be married and never say anything of any importance to one another? But outsiders don't grasp the essence of this relationship. This man and woman *have* communicated. Now, they know each other. They're comfortable with each other. That's what's important to them.

Now if I as a stranger come in and say, "Well, hold on a minute. What do you mean, you're comfortable with each other? That's not enough! You should be experiencing the interchange of new ideas! Why don't you have some meaningful conversations?" the couple might answer, "We have nothing to say to each other. But we're comfortable."

"Yes, but that's not right," I might say.

Well, it *is* right—for them. The point is, who am I to come in and say that these people should be changing

151

their relationship, or that they should be experiencing this, or doing that? At least they go to bed at night and sleep a good sleep. They know that when they wake up in the morning, they have the support and love of the person beside them, whether they talk about something new or not. That person is *there*. And while they don't have the highs that some relationships do, they don't have the lows either. There's something to be said for this kind of steady, secure, long-term bond. After all, think about what it would be like to have all your relationship-related pain gone, as well as all the insecurity, anger, and depression. Even if, in the process, you had to give up all your relationship-related superhighs, the idea might still be tempting.

This kind of trade-off is what makes some Adaptive Supportive relationships so long-lasting. They don't really have the lows or the highs. They're just kind of driving along at fifty-five miles per hour. They don't go fifty-six, and, even if you took away the speed limit, they never would. Nor do they ever have to pull over to the side and stop because they've broken down, or because they feel an urge to ask themselves why they're on this journey in the first place. No, they just keep tooling along with the kind of steadiness that constitutes part of the strong undergirding of the Adaptive Supportive world.

When it comes to friendships, Adaptive Supportives form strong and long-lasting ones. They are honest enough to tell a friend what they are thinking and feeling. And they demand very little of their friends, except for the trust and loyalty that they so readily give themselves. Those who can return these qualities will have a friend for life in an Adaptive Supportive. On the high side of their energy they are caring, supportive, giving, and concerned. While these qualities may be somewhat hidden if an Adaptive Supportive is not actualizing the high side of his or her energy, the friendship can still be very solid if the Adaptive Supportive has a good sense of self. The friendship will be comforting and noncompetitive, allowing both parties to relax and be themselves.

Relationships with family members can be more complex. The family unit is important to Adaptive Supportives, and they devote a lot of their time and energy to family members. They can be loyal, giving, and highly protective parents. The problem is, their sometimes rigid view of life can make them especially judgmental of the people closest to them. Adaptive Supportives want to pass on to their children the same conditioning they themselves received, and they expect their children to share all their beliefs without question. As a result, the children may feel there is little room for them to explore different avenues in life. Eventually, they may rebel against the family to break free of its rigid doctrines and escape their parents' preconceived notions of how they should live their lives.

In fact, children who grow up in an Adaptive Supportive home may end up taking a radically different approach to life than their parents did. As teenagers they start to sense that their family life is not dynamic in any way—their parents are not challenging authority, for example, or attempting to make positive changes in their lives. The children start to feel that they are in a cultural, political, and religious prison. When they break free, the new route they choose in life may depend entirely on the influence of their peers.

Energy Combinations

As for life energy combinations, Adaptive Supportives tend to be happiest when they're not overwhelmed by the other party in the relationship. So a Dynamic Aggressive, in particular, would not be a good bet for a relationship with a member of this soft, easily manipulated energy group. In fact, in the long term, a kind of slavery might result from this pairing. Nor would an Adaptive Aggressive be a terribly promising partner. These are the people who figure out all the angles and then go on to use them, and there's just too much of a chance that the more naive Adaptive Supportive would be opportunistically used—and as a result hurt—especially when you're looking at a many-years-long relationship, which is the kind that Adaptive Supportives generally want.

A relationship with a Dynamic Assertive has some possibilities. The Adaptive Supportive can live vicariously through the activities of the Dynamic Assertive, and the latter can gain needed love and support from his or her quieter partner. The dangers here: The Adaptive Supportive may find the whole thing too intense, and the Dynamic Assertive may get bored. So it's good if the two don't spend too much time together!

Of course, since Adaptive Supportives tend to place a premium on togetherness, at least in terms of physical proximity, this might be a problem. Thus members of other, less intimidating energy groups are generally the best candidates for partnership with an Adaptive Supportive. Prime among these are Adaptive Supportives themselves. Two Adaptive Supportives together, and on their up side, can form a beautiful, uncomplicated, decades-long relationship that comes as close to the "happily ever after" image of fairy tales as anything else on this planet. Such a relationship satisfies the needs of both partners for security and permanence, and what's more, it can produce some well-adjusted, happy children—no small feat in today's world. Other realistic possibilities for the Adaptive Supportive are the Dynamic Supportive (that most "laid back" of the Dynamics) and the Adaptive Assertive. An Adaptive Supportive and a Creative Assertive sometimes do well too, although the Creative's mood and activity swings may not be easily tolerated. With this particular combination you have two people progressing through life at completely different rhythms. The Adaptive Supportive tends to plod along, while the Creative leaps, bounds, races, and then stalls. So these two, together, would not be exactly synchronized!

THE WORLD'S MOST IMPORTANT WORKERS

Adaptive Supportives generally do functional work. They may be clerical-level employees or blue-collar workers in government agencies or factories. They may work at the checkout counters in retail establishments or at construction sites. Rarely do Adaptive Supportives seek out positions of responsibility. Instead, they may look for ways to exercise some control over their immediate work environment.

Sometimes other energy types make the mistake of judging Adaptive Supportives by the social status of the work they do. They make value judgments about people based on their position in life, the number of degrees they have earned, or the amount of money they have accumulated. But to do so is to ignore the fact that any given job, when done correctly and with pride, is equal to all others because it contributes to society. All the parts work as a whole, creating an essential balance that makes life better for everyone.

For instance, postal workers are generally not found on the cover of *People* magazine; they're not "important" enough. But a post office worker is suddenly very important when you need your mail. Likewise, a construction worker is important when you need a building to live in, and a sanitation worker, who toils to keep your environment clean, could be the most important person to you in terms of your health. In fact, he's probably a lot more vital to your life than many of the faces on magazine covers.

Indeed, Adaptive Supportives play an absolutely essential role in our culture, as in any. Without them the inner workings of society would simply cease to function. Those who denigrate functional workers have a limited understanding of value, and they grossly downplay our mutual need and interdependence. The Dynamic energies need the cooperation of Adaptive Supportives, just as Adaptive Supportives can benefit from the leadership of Dynamics and the artistic efforts of Creative Assertives.

On their up side, Adaptive Supportives are conscientious and responsible workers who take their jobs seriously. Many, in fact, are highly skilled and talented craftspeople. They take great pride in the quality of their work, and they continually seek to improve and perfect their skills. What's more, they respect the notion of excellence in general, and appreciate it in others' work as well as in their own.

A strength of this group is that if you show an Adaptive Supportive the right way to do a particular job, once he or she masters it, that person will continue to do the job at the same high level consistently. I've seen this phenomenon with such workers as gardeners and school crossing guards, who will continue to put themselves out week after week and year after year to make every element in the garden fit exactly into specifications, or to make sure that no child crosses the street until all traffic is at an absolute standstill. With Adaptive Supportive workers on the high end of their energy, slacking off is a concept that just doesn't apply.

Of course, the Adaptive Supportive gardener will not be the one to try unusual color combinations or let the hedge grow to some unorthodox height in order to experiment with a new sun/shade pattern. You'd need a Creative Assertive gardener for that. Likewise, the Adaptive Supportive crossing guard won't be the one to launch a campaign for a town bike path, whereas a Dynamic Assertive might. The thing is, if you put members of these other groups in the respective jobs, they probably won't stay with the work as long as an Adaptive Supportive will. Nor will you have the same measure of self-administered quality control.

But on the down side, Adaptive Supportives often erect artificial barriers to the personal growth that would give them more opportunities in the workplace. They may dislike their jobs, but they won't seek the education, training, or experience needed to do something more interesting. In many cases they simply do what they must to get by and earn a paycheck. In essence they trade off opportunity for job security—an aspect of work life that has tremendous value to Adaptive Supportives.

A pitfall for this group is that their desire to explore life will peak early on, generally in high school or soon thereafter. Many then lose their motivation to grow professionally and personally. They begin to dwell on past achievements as a way to sublimate their frustration with the boredom of their present life. Adaptive Supportives often gather to talk about the "glory days" when they excelled at a sport in high school, for instance. They can become consumed by these remembrances, repeating the same stories tirelessly to a group of close friends. But rarely do they want to look at their present situation to identify opportunities for change and growth.

As a result, Adaptive Supportives can become spectators in life. They begin to live vicariously through others, by watching soap operas and movies, or reading tabloids. It's as if they believe adventure is something to be created and experienced by others, not something available in their own lives. Adaptive Supportives even begin to identify with other spectators who share their interests, such as the fans of a particular sports team or famous personality. In essence, they look for positive reinforcement and a sense of self in such spectator groups.

PERSONAL CHANGE IS NOT COMFORTABLE

Adaptive Supportives have a difficult time with change, and this is true just as much on an individual level as on a social or political one. Many are so attached to their beliefs and lifestyle that they cannot conceive of questioning those precepts, let alone moving beyond them for a new direction in life. They may change the circumstances of their day-to-day existence—their jobs, houses, or even family and friends—but they don't change themselves.

There's no denying that personal growth requires awareness, effort, and commitment. It requires a willingness to consider all sides of an issue; to take chances in life; and, in the end, to make constructive changes. While Adaptive Supportives may perceive that there is more to life than they were led to believe, they're generally afraid to jeopardize what they already have to go out and pursue it. That would mean stepping outside their models of belief—an action that is sure to cause some discomfort.

Indeed, Adaptive Supportives tend to deny their capacity for intellectual growth, particularly as they age, and particularly when they are on the down side of their energy curve. They don't trust their ability to grow because they might have to deny what they currently are in the process of doing. It's all a little too difficult and frightening, so self-awareness is not something they move toward. The end result is that they may deny re-

159

sponsibility for themselves in every way—for their emotional health, their spiritual health, and their physical health as well. This is the group that says, about death, "When your number's up, your number's up," and they're convinced that there's nothing they can do to forestall that. After a certain number of years of this kind of fatalism and denial, any capacity for personal change or growth dwindles to nothingness.

To revive this capacity, Adaptive Supportives must recognize that there is nothing intrinsic about them that prevents personal growth. Despite all their beliefs and fears, which can indeed be stifling, they—just like everyone else—are capable of change. But they have to take charge of their own development. They can't wait for some big boss figure to give them permission to change, to say it's okay. This waiting for permission is a major stumbling block for many Adaptive Supportives. They wait for a signal from some higher up before they begin to make any major transition.

The few Adaptive Supportives who do break through this "big-boss barrier" become very excited about their own untapped potential. Once they start the process of personal growth, they open themselves up to new experiences and new ways of viewing their lives. The catch is that they may need someone to work with them—generally a more dynamic personality—to keep them motivated and to supply structure and direction. Provided they have that guidance, they will continue to develop their potential.

WHO ARE YOU? ONLY *YOU* KNOW

In the end, Adaptive Supportives are capable of substantial transitions when they break out of society's mold and reach the high side of their energy. With the right catalyst to encourage them, they will extricate themselves from bad marriages, bad jobs, and other types of harmful circumstances. But they have to be willing to let go of their fears and to face change as a positive event.

If you're an Adaptive Supportive you may lose sight of the following: No other human being—not your parents, spouse, siblings, best friends, political leader, or clergy—has the right to tell you who you are. No one has the right to limit your choices in life and diminish your individuality. If you put too much stock in other people's definition of who you are, you may begin to believe them and even become dependent on their approval and feedback. After a while you can find yourself needing someone else to "rubber-stamp" everything you do.

The definition of the real self comes from within. It's up to you to recognize who you are and to take responsibility for your own well-being. While the support and acceptance of others give life a pleasant and comfortable quality, you shouldn't let a need for security prevent you from seeking out your higher self.

Beyond that, you need to question the notion that stability and permanence are the most important qualities in life. They definitely have their place, but so does the process of change. Look at the way you are living and try to determine if it has real meaning for you. Think about the work you do, the relationships you form, and the values you express daily. Are you happy with these aspects of your life? If not, give yourself the freedom to try some new ideas and to attempt some new physical, mental, and spiritual approaches to the challenge of daily living.

And above all, recognize that the beliefs that have been handed down to you by others are not necessarily the beliefs you should accept and adhere to in life. Yes, they *may* be the right beliefs for you. Or they may be 99 percent right for you, or 75 percent, or 50 percent. The point is, beliefs are something you can accept or reject, whole or piecemeal, and it's every human's right to do so.

You don't have to be a revolutionary. Stridency and committing acts that will get you on the six-o'clock news may not be your style. Still, you can work within our society's institutions without relinquishing your power and control to those who run them. What it boils down to, in the end, is that you don't want to end up disillusioned and disappointed in your old age because you accepted someone else's prescription for living as the only possible one. There are so many ways to live. Decide what values are important to you and your family, and then define yourself according to what you truly believe.

GUARDIANS OF ORDER
AND STABILITY:
ADAPTIVE ASSERTIVES

There is a small subgroup of the Adaptive Supportive energy type that shares this type's strong need to fit in with the majority but that differs from the type in that its members will take on limited leadership roles. This subgroup is the Adaptive Assertives, and it's a group that's distinguished by having some of the most fulfilled, least dysfunctional members of society. Adaptive Assertives, like their close energy cousins the Adaptive Supportives, mold themselves to society's expectations and live within the social contract they are given. The difference is that Adaptive Assertives will challenge wrongs within their immediate environment. Unlike Adaptive Supportives, who accept things just as they are, Adaptive Assertives try to correct problems within the system. In that way they have an assertive component to their natural energy.

An Adaptive Assertive might be the unionized

worker who challenges corruption at the top of the union, the farmer who chooses to "go organic," the neighbor who encourages others to get involved in preventive health, or the parent who tries to improve the local school system. These people are in a sense leaders within their own social and work environments, although at times they are following the lead of Dynamic Assertives within those environments, or working in tandem with them. The thing that distinguishes the Adaptive Assertive orientation from that of Dynamic Assertives is that Adaptive Assertives are not interested in challenging whole systems; they're just trying to right a wrong, or to correct a flaw, within a small microcosm of a system. They remain obedient in that they don't question the big picture—the larger issues of how our world view might be improved or how society is organized. As Adaptives they do what society asks of them, whether it be joining the army, voting the party line, or keeping their front lawn trimmed to an acceptable height.

Nonetheless, Adaptive Assertives are smart, idealistic, and conscientious people. On the high side of their energy they play just as important a role in society as any other energy type. Adaptive Assertives are often willing to facilitate change on a personal scale, and their constructive efforts feed into the larger forces for change. They form bonds with other energy types to help make the world work better and more honestly. They may be more predictable than those with the Dynamic energies, but their high-side efforts are useful and positive.

In short, Adaptive Assertives are superb pragmatists. While Dynamic Assertives may be able to offer more sophisticated critiques of what's wrong with various societal paradigms, Adaptive Assertives will actually get down in the trenches to make one particular corner of society run well. They'll do the fact-gathering that's necessary to keep any enterprise running optimally. For instance, an Adaptive Assertive at a school board meeting might show up armed with specific information on which grades lack textbooks for what subjects, and where in the budget the money for these might be found.

Since they're willing and able to deal with the nitty-gritty of change in a limited, familiar sphere, Adaptive Assertives excel in supervisory positions. In this group you'll find people who aren't afraid of detail work and who can use it to effect positive results—people such as foremen, department heads, school principals, police chiefs, and engineers. All of these occupations require highly developed organizational ability, which is generally an Adaptive Assertive forte.

IN TUNE, ON TOP . . . INTOLERANT?

When they're living on the high side of their energy, Adaptive Assertives focus on making the best of what they have. In fact, members of this group are often the most fulfilled and happy of all the energy types. This makes sense when you consider the following: This world as we know it is basically an Adaptive's world—that is, however much the visionary Dynamics or dreamy Creatives might want to change things, at any given time, except perhaps for a short period after a revolution, the world we're living in is the status-quo world of the powers that be. It's an imperfect world that has to be adapted to. And who better to enjoy that than the Adaptive Assertive? All the Dynamics, and the Creatives, as we've said, are perpetually itching to change things; they're too idealistic to be consistently happy. As for the Adaptives, the Adaptive Supportive usually has too little control of his or her work and economic life to be really fulfilled. And the Adaptive Aggressive, although often well off economically, is by nature a constantly striving person, always seeking the next big opportunity for a power play; this predatory lifestyle doesn't make for long-term happiness either.

But the Adaptive Assertive doesn't have these roadblocks on the way to contentment. In the Adaptive Assertive you have someone who's in tune with prevailing values; someone who's generally on top of things workwise, in that he or she may have a supervisory post and thus some measure of control; and someone who's not power-hungry. So there's a greater potential for happiness in this group than in the others.

These are family-oriented and civic-minded people who attempt to do something constructive within the boundaries society has set. They seek creative outlets for their ideas, and they take pride in living an autonomous and highly principled life. When they are on the high side of their energy they will have a healthy home, a healthy family, and a healthy workplace. What's more, the world around them will be a better place for their efforts.

A lot of high-end qualities of the Adaptive Assertive are the qualities we think of as traditional, conservative virtues—"the things that made America great." Thrift, punctuality, hard work, honesty, persistence—all of these bring to mind Ben Franklin's aphorisms, and Adaptive Assertives on their high side. We can laugh at these "nerdy" attributes, but we do so at our own peril, because without them we'd have no viable workplaces, schools, or neighborhoods. We'd have no PTAs, Elks Lodges, Boy or Girl Scouts, or any of the other non-glamorous organizations that work to keep our civilization civil.

One of the adages we can probably all remember from our youth is "A stitch in time saves nine." Adaptive Assertives have taken this seriously in that they tend to be excellent at planning ahead, taking steps to forestall any potential disaster. Thus this is the group whose members hardly ever declare bankruptcy. They're good savers, family-budget makers, and buyers of insurance. You hardly ever see an Adaptive Assertive operating in a crisis mode. They don't have to—they've planned for every eventuality.

Saving for the future is one of those traditional American activities that seems to have gone out of fashion in some circles, but not with Adaptive Assertives. Others may squander everything they earn in a quest for immediate gratification, but members of this energy group are still firm believers in the virtue of systematically saving for their children's education, their own retirement, or that proverbial rainy day. So Adaptive Assertives aid the national economy by being this country's "master savers." And they're "master buyers" as well, in that they pride themselves on being educated consumers who research the market before making purchases so they can get high quality at the best price. They eschew both schlocky goods at rock-bottom prices, and the extravagant. In their shopping habits, as in much else in

Adaptive Assertives' lives, moderation is the preferred mode.

If you're trying to think of Adaptive Assertives you know, and none stands out in your mind, that may actually be a result of another of this group's attributes: They don't stand out. Members of this energy group are basically humble, nonflashy people who have no desire to call attention to themselves. They tend to dress and house themselves conservatively, and are happy to live calmly according to their principles, letting others create the noise, crises, and drama of life.

But the quiet quality of this group does not mean they are pushovers. Adaptive Assertives are idealistic people who value order and justice and who will work to clean up an environment where order and justice seem lacking. So on their high side, Adaptive Assertives serve as the conscience of a particular environment—the watchdogs who want to keep it honest and make it all it should be. They are very connected to their communities—where they often live their entire lives—and have a natural inclination to protect their own neighborhoods. They are the ones who would say to others, "We have to deal with this problem. It's our neighborhood, it's our jobs, it's our community—let's keep it healthy." In this respect they serve as role models for others by showing them that change is a worthy and achievable goal.

On the down side, a facet of this group that can be problematic is that Adaptive Assertives are not particularly tolerant. This is a highly functional group—good at coping with reality, working hard, feeling reasonably contented with what they have, and planning for a rainy day. So they sometimes have trouble understanding why others can't always operate in the same way and achieve the same things they have. "Why can't they work hard like I did?" they'll ask about the poor, or "What do they want, anyway?" they'll ask about a group with a political grievance they can't quite comprehend.

The trouble is that Adaptive Assertives, while good with detail, are not all that practiced in their imagination skills. So they sometimes have trouble imagining how someone could have grown up in different circumstances than they did, with different gifts or liabilities, or even with totally different values. Some of these suppositions are beyond their ken, and so an Adaptive Assertive on his down side is capable of dismissing individuals, or even whole groups of people, as "lazy," "weird," or even "no damn good."

"LET'S DO IT RIGHT!"

One of the most distinguishing characteristics of Adaptive Assertives is that they believe in doing things correctly. They don't just want to get a job done—they want to get it done right. This energy type is responsible for upholding the quality and dependability of many American products; in fact, where they've been permitted to, Adaptive Assertives have helped stem industrial degeneration in this country by taking enormous pride in the quality of their work. They approach their jobs with professionalism, and they can be especially effective as supervisors or foremen who pass their high standards on to others in the company, specifically the Adaptive Supportives who are working just beneath them.

BETTER HOMES AND GARDENS

The Adaptive Assertive's strong desire to do things the right way is also reflected in his or her home environment. Their homes tend to be sensibly decorated, sparkling clean, and organized to the hilt. These are the people who have a place for everything, and everything is in its place. What's more, everything works, and if it doesn't, it's repaired immediately. There's a meticulous quality to the Adaptive Assertive's approach to life, and it shows.

Take a top-to-bottom, inside-and-out tour of the Adaptive Assertive's house and you see order everywhere: In the attic, old suitcases are piled in size-place order. So are old magazines, with chronological order entering in here as well. In the bedrooms, mattresses are rotated on a schedule, so that no part gets unduly worn. There are wall thermometers in each bedroom as an accuracy check for the thermostat thermometers (and if one of the wall thermometers was wrongly calibrated so it reads a couple of degrees too low, if you took that one off the wall you would see this fact penciled neatly on the back). In the bathrooms, toothpaste tubes are rolled up from the bottom and towels (color-coordinated with the tile) are stacked on a shelf with the folded edges all facing out.

The kitchen? Hospitals could look to it as a model of antisepsis. And note that there's nothing random about the placement of magnets on the refrigerator. In the living room—well, you may not be allowed to sit in it, but if you were, you wouldn't see or inhale a speck of dust. The dining room (it *was* dined in once!) could pass the white-glove test too. In the basement, well-cared-for tools are all hung up on hooks—*labeled* hooks. Outside, the flower garden is a perfect rainbow of color surrounded by a knockout lawn; in fact, the whole yard is a showplace, and that includes the doghouse—the inside! And the yard, like the house, is kept up daily, even hourly. Soon after it snows, each flake is dutifully transferred from where it doesn't belong to where it's permitted, and ditto for the errant leaves of fall. You could make fun of neatnik Adaptive Assertives ad infinitum, but on the other hand, they're responsible for a lot of the beauty and stability found in neighborhoods all across this country.

By the way, concerning the Adaptive Assertive's prompt repairing of what's broken, he or she often will not have to wait for the repairman, because he can fix it himself. This group has a high percentage of superb, intuitive mechanics who can figure out how to fix almost anything. What's more, Adaptive Assertives often enjoy helping others to the extent that they'll gladly tackle neighbors' minor household emergencies—gratis.

I had an uncle who exemplified this. Whenever he found out that a neighbor or relative had something that had broken down in or around that person's house, he made it a point to fix it. And he didn't make a big deal about this either. He simply showed up at the person's house as soon as he could fit it into his schedule and, without fanfare, fixed the thing. He didn't need any helpers—he seemed to like working alone—and he would never accept money or any other payment for his

171

efforts. To those relatives with no mechanical ability, this Adaptive Assertive uncle was a godsend!

And one might say that he was a godsend in another sense. You see, it was this same uncle who, if you were homebound, would keep you supplied, weekly, and for the rest of your life, with a copy of the minister's latest sermon. And he certainly wouldn't accept payment for that service either. Payment would have been beside the point anyway, the point being that my uncle just wanted to keep things in order, to keep things humming.

LOYAL TO THE END—WITH SOME STRINGS ATTACHED

Adaptive Assertives generally do not come across as warm people, but they can be loving to their family members. In fact, family life is very important to the Adaptive Assertives. They tend to center their lives around these relationships, socializing with siblings, cousins, aunts, and uncles, for example, more often than with coworkers or others outside the family.

An Adaptive Assertive can be a good friend to a select group of people. They don't tend to form a lot of friendships, and in many cases they have the same friends throughout their entire lives. Once they bond with certain people, they remain true to those relationships. An Adaptive Assertive would never betray a friendship; like their Adaptive Supportive counterparts, they are exceptionally loyal people.

The drawback is that Adaptive Assertives generally expect others to behave in a prescribed fashion. They have been conditioned to accept society's manners and morals, and they expect others to adhere to those same standards. That doesn't leave a lot of room for individuality and warmth in their relationships. However, Adaptive Assertives can form lifelong and loving relationships with those who share their beliefs.

Many Adaptive Assertives also develop relationships through their civic activities. They are likely to be Scout leaders, for example, or to serve as elders in their churches. They are conscientious people who will perform volunteer work for organizations that help the homebound or elderly in their communities. While there is the tendency of Adaptive Assertives to come across as too opinionated or intolerant, if others can accept these idiosyncrasies, they will benefit from the checks and balances that Adaptive Assertives provide in their immediate environments.

Energy Combinations

An Adaptive Assertive and an Adaptive Supportive, sharing similar energies and attitudes as they do, can form a solid relationship, as can two Adaptive Assertives. In the latter case, an interesting situation sometimes develops: With an Adaptive Assertive couple you get a very stable, ordered, mutually supportive unit in which doing things right becomes such an art form that, after a while, the rest of humanity begins to look wrong to the couple. They can develop an "us against the world" mindset, and their union can evolve into something quite insular and intolerant. But their house always looks great—and they're happy together!

A coupling with a drastically lower chance of mutual satisfaction would be an Adaptive Assertive and a Creative Assertive. These two don't tend to attract each other, but if they did get together, it's not hard to imagine the troublesome scenario that would follow. The Creative would shortly come to feel stifled by all the Adaptive Assertive's rules, which would probably run the gamut from not putting your feet on the coffee table to the necessity of earning a living. As for the Adaptive Assertive, she or he would soon be disgusted by the Creative's erratic schedule, moods, housekeeping, etc. No, these two, paired, would not be happy campers!

PERSONAL GROWTH—WITHIN LIMITS

There are two main factors that put a damper on personal growth for Adaptive Assertives. One is that, as the energy group experiencing the most life satisfaction, Adaptive Assertives don't feel the impetus to change as much as others might. This is understandable: If you're happy with life, you don't want to upset the applecart unnecessarily. Of course, you don't want to remain totally stagnant either, and Adaptive Assertives on their high side *are* willing to grow intellectually and spiritually. For example, they might stay abreast of issues relating to preventive health and use the information to make constructive changes in their lives, such as supporting organic farmers in their local communities, growing some of their own food in the backyard, taking vitamins, or adding an air purifier to their homes.

The other main factor working against growth in this

energy group is the Adaptive Assertive's tremendous need for order and security in life. Given this aspect of their energy, their growth patterns tend to be circular, covering the same ground upon which they have always felt familiar. In essence, Adaptive Assertives stay within the social and work systems that define their lives, rather than reaching out to experience something totally new or connecting with the larger contexts in life.

If you're an Adaptive Assertive, then, change at a broader level is not going to come naturally. But you might want to consider this: It's fine to focus on correcting the wrongs within your own circles. After all, these are problems that others may overlook because they are not affected by them. However, it pays to at least occasionally look beyond the inner workings of your particular milieu to examine the very nature of a system itself. In addition to having minor, localized flaws that need fine-tuning, the systems you have come to accept may have larger-scale limitations that need to be addressed. By learning to question these systems you could promote your own personal growth, as well as further enhance the important role you play in society's progression toward constructive change.

ADAPTIVE AGGRESSIVES— THE FACILITATORS

You can call them opportunists. They are. But you can also say that Adaptive Aggressives are resourceful, socially aware people with a keen sense of where their interests lie. They are goal-oriented, long-term planners who are drawn to people they believe have the power or capacity to help them reach their goals. Bottom line, they are survivors. As professionals, they may be top-management advisers, lawyers, sales and marketing people, actors and actresses, office managers, or lieutenants in the military.

You can call them climbers. They are. But you can say, too, that Adaptive Assertives are bright people who bring vitality, joy, and a sense of openness and healthy acquisitiveness to life. They know what they want and they go out and get it, and this aggressive go-getter spirit can be a refreshing thing—provided it's not cloaked in deception. If an Adaptive Aggressive is up-front about his or her ambition, and if he maintains a general standard of honesty, it can be an exhilarating experience to be around him. In fact this is the wildest and most exciting energy type—bar none. Yes, the Dynamic Aggressive shares the strong drive of the Adaptive Aggressive, but in the Dynamic the drive is more focused; it tends to be tailored to a specific goal. The Adaptive Aggressive, on the other hand, is more restless and all over the place with his drive. He'll try anything!

Adaptive Aggressives often seek power and status, but they are not dynamic creators themselves. Thus, on their down side, they may lack confidence in their own abilities and turn to other people for focus and ideas. They become attuned to what others need or enjoy and try to make themselves indispensable to these people by fulfilling their every desire. Adaptive Aggressives have an ever-present need to be accepted; thus they may behave like emotional chameleons by adopting the beliefs and ideas of the person they identify with at the moment.

In many cases Adaptive Aggressives are driven people who have not been appreciated for themselves. They lack self-assurance and a sense of grounding in their own individuality, perhaps because they learned early on to become what others wanted. Their emotions go up, down, and all around, depending on how secure they feel in the situation of the moment. Despite this emotional volatility, though, they try to present themselves in a dignified and controlled manner.

Adaptive Aggressives can be so hypersensitive to criticism that they cannot bear to consider their own shortcomings. On their down side, in fact, they generally are not interested in improving themselves, other than to upgrade their external circumstances. Nor do they have a capacity for self-observation—they are too outwardly focused. They may appear to have a strong ego, but what they actually have is a strong persona.

Adaptive Aggressives' attachments are often based on neediness, and because others are instrumental in making them feel significant, members of this energy group tend to blame others when they don't feel good about themselves. This can be frustrating for everyone involved. Also, the personal lives of those with this life energy are often cluttered and chaotic because they hang on to their emotions, their past, and their pain. But they disguise this pain because they believe they must hide their vulnerability.

When other people interact with an Adaptive Aggressive, they must use all their senses and their intuition to determine what the Adaptive Aggressive is feeling and how he or she is responding to them. Is the response honest? Or is it less than honest? Adaptive Aggressives may believe for the moment that they are being sincere, but if any group can fool a lie detector it is this one because they have an adeptness at self-deception as well as at deceiving others. Sometimes their deceit consists not so much of out-and-out lying as it does of lying by omission, or of exaggeration or rationalization. This group has a great ability to rationalize, and it is one they make full use of. Of course, others eventually realize that the Adaptive Aggressive is playing fast and loose with the facts. Hopefully this realization comes before too much harm has been done.

An Adaptive Aggressive on the down side does not develop an internal set of values that remains stable across all situations. Their integrity is linked to the momentary standards of the person or situation to which they have attached themselves. Thus they tend to be unpredictable and skittish. They will end something very quickly if they are betrayed. In fact, they may even expect to be betrayed, because they do not trust others easily. At the same time, they may fear losing what they have if they believe it is the best they can do for the moment. These kinds of strategic considerations are always on their minds.

In fact, strategy and planning are key to this energy group, with other people playing an instrumental role in their plans. Whether this role is a witting or an unwitting one depends—as so much does for this group—on the circumstances. In other words, sometimes Adaptive Aggressives will let you in on their plans, and sometimes they won't. If they believe that informing you will help them, they will let you in on the plan. If they think you might resent it, they won't; they are masters of the hidden agenda. In any event, they are savvy people who see all that is around them. They can see the big picture and develop short- and long-term goals within its framework.

Adaptive Aggressives take advantage of every opportunity, and not only that—they make opportunities happen. That's why salespeople are often Adaptive Aggressives: This type has the chutzpah to walk into a place and get someone interested in their product or service. On their up side they are energetic and highly effective in the sales field, but on the down side they may go for the cheap approach. If this tactic fails, they tend to make excuses for themselves.

While, occupationally, Adaptive Aggressives may be good as salespeople, in life they sometimes seem more like shoppers—comparison shoppers. That is to say, Adaptive Aggressives are constantly comparing what they have to what they see around them, be it in the personal or the professional area. Then they'll shop around for the better opportunity. Why are they always on the lookout for something better? It's usually because they're unhappy, insecure in themselves. The irony is that to other people, Adaptive Aggressives often appear to have a secure, or even cushy, environment. But for them it's always only temporary.

Adaptive Aggressives tend to be clandestine because they sense their weaknesses may be exposed and they'll be "found out." On their down side, then, they may lie, cheat, manipulate, and execute all manner of power plays to pit people against each other. The goal of these low-side machinations is a hidden but desperate urge to protect their image, as well as what they have, and they're not likely to feel remorse when operating in this mode.

Adaptive Aggressives are shrewd socially in that they're familiar with the social scene and know how to use it, and they've mastered enough etiquette to be able to maneuver smoothly through various situations. Also, you almost never see an Adaptive Aggressive who's not dressed properly. Whatever the occasion, they've got the image down. For instance, if they're in the office they'll be dressed to precisely the level of formality the boss favors; if they're working out they'll have on whatever exercisewear is currently in vogue; not for them the old shorts and T-shirt that just happen to be in the drawer. For a weekend at someone's country retreat they'll be sporting just the right mix of the casual and the costly. Others at the retreat may use the weekend to become at one with nature, but it can look as if the Adaptive Aggressive is more at one with the fashion ads!

Because they are concerned with appearances, Adaptive Aggressives give the impression that they have control over their energy. But there's a frenetic quality to that energy, unlike that of other people who combine a high energy level with a certain calmness. The Adaptive Aggressive's energy tends to be turbulent. In a serene setting, such as that country retreat, the Adaptive Aggressive's inability to relax really shows up. She will sit for a moment, start to fidget, read one page of a book, put the book down, turn on the radio, walk around the room for a while. Then she might go into the other room, pick up the phone but have no one to call, watch a movie, get something to eat, walk around the grounds, but be spooked by the quiet. People in this energy group are not ones to appreciate quiet; in fact, they're sometimes scared by it. Returning to her room, the Adaptive Aggressive might try to nap, give up on that idea, turn on the TV, consult her schedule of trains back to the city.

Even in ordinary circumstances, Adaptive Aggressives always seem to have a surplus of energy. When you're in a room with them, you can never forget that they're there because they're tapping their feet or pacing or even saying things to themselves under their breath. Adaptive Aggressives sometimes have a bull-in-a-china-shop quality to them that can make them uncomfortable to be around—unless you're up for a prolonged, intense energy jolt.

If you are, then it's another story. An Adaptive Aggressive can motivate you as no one else can. A Dynamic Aggressive or Assertive may inspire you, but an Adaptive Aggressive can get you chomping at the bit and primed for action; it's as if they have a surplus of adrenaline flow that—if you're receptive—somehow transfers itself to you. Members of this group make great athletic coaches for this reason.

One reason Adaptive Aggressives are often restless and troubled is that their sense of self is so fluid. They depend in an ongoing way on interaction with externals to keep them from feeling unsettling emotions. When they stop moving, planning, and scheming, they are frightened by the emptiness and insecurity they feel. These feelings drive them onward, toward the next goal. And when that one is reached, then there's the next; they're like the ever-swimming shark, unable to stop.

When frustrated, Adaptive Aggressives tend to react impulsively. They blame their frustration on others, and they may live in a state of turmoil that embroils those around them. Neither do they handle stress well. In a crisis situation, Adaptive Aggressives tend to panic. As a prisoner of war, for example, an Adaptive Aggressive might fold immediately and volunteer information about others in his group.

The Adaptive Aggressive woman is an emotional chameleon; she can adapt to any person or environment. You like Italian food? She does, too. You like the opera? She's an old opera buff. You'd like to go to France? Best country in the world for her. No matter what your needs or desires, this type of woman will adapt to them and reflect those needs herself. (It should be noted that up to at least the 1960s, young women were trained—by teen and women's magazines, and by the prevailing wisdom—to be exactly these sort of mental and emotional mirrors of their dates' and mates' frames of mind. For instance, to be popular with boys, girls were supposed to find out what their dates were interested in and then get interested in it themselves—or pretend to be; that would do, too. So there's no doubt that some of today's Adaptive Aggressive women are the products of pervasive social conditioning a few decades back.)

Many Adaptive Aggressive women have a hidden agenda. In other words, they adapt themselves to you for a time, all the while getting what they can from you until it benefits them to move on. Perhaps they can no longer obtain what they need from you, they think they are going to be exposed, or someone better comes along. And if a man should discover that an Adaptive Aggressive woman does not belong in his life, she will no doubt make him pay for having been involved with her at all.

The Adaptive Aggressive woman can be exciting and even scary. Think of the character played by Glenn Close in *Fatal Attraction*. That's that Adaptive Aggressive woman on her down side. On the up side, an Adaptive Aggressive woman would have enjoyed that same experience without degenerating to the point of vindictiveness. In fact, the Adaptive Aggressive woman is generally controlled, self-assured, independent, and methodical on the high side of her energy. She's a great person to work with because she's not afraid to assert herself and take charge. She has more confidence than any of the other energy types when it comes to dealing with people. She will get a job done right.

Likewise, Adaptive Aggressive men have strong personalities, and, on the surface at least, they are committed to their beliefs. They are determined, organized, nononsense people. They can bring order to a disorganized environment, fix something that is not working, and offer good ideas on how to resolve a problem. As a result, they make excellent management advisers, office managers, and sales and marketing people. But on the down side there may be no virtue they hold sacred. Thus the Adaptive Aggressive male can become self-interested, manipulative, and conniving.

These men can survive anywhere due to their adaptive nature. Put them in any environment, positive or negative, and they will adjust to the conditions by mirroring the needs and desires of the people around them. Take Oliver North, a perfect example of an Adaptive Aggressive on his down side. North did what he believed was right because he honored the authority of his superiors. He adapted to the situation in which he found himself and the problem he was presented with. Nor did he betray the people behind him when the situation was exposed. In fact, others betrayed him. Like any Adaptive Aggressive, North was dismayed when the people he protected made a scapegoat of him.

Ronald Reagan was a Dynamic Assertive on the down side. But he surrounded himself with Adaptive Aggressives such as Attorney General Meese and others who could hide his limitations and serve as the brains, mouth, and conscience behind the president's actions. We should remember that a Dynamic who holds public office will almost always have strong Adaptive Aggressives behind him. These behind-the-scenes people pull the strings, and they are the ones we must identify and watch.

Hitler, for example, was a shrewd, clever, and powerful man, but he was not intelligent. He, too, supported himself with strong and intelligent people such as Joseph Goebbels, who had several Ph.D.s. Even institutions such as the Catholic Church have leaders who are powerful, clever, and ruthless. Pope Leo X was not smart, but he surrounded himself with insiders who could serve as his voice.

Many actors and actresses are Adaptive Aggressives who can excite others by the ability to take on any emotion and mimic any attitude. That adaptability is a unique part of their energy, and, used in the show business arena, it's a positive thing, a far cry from the schemings and manipulations that characterize some Adaptive Aggressives' use of their energy.

IN CHARGE OF THEIR ENERGY— OR RULED BY IT?

When operating on the high end, Adaptive Aggressives will get in charge of their energy so they don't burn out and resort to using other people. In this phase they are exciting, supportive, and spontaneous. They take a constructive approach to anything they do. On the down side they do burn out and use themselves up, as well as others. There is a wide range between these two extremes, and an Adaptive Aggressive's position along this spectrum will depend on his or her conditioning and the influence of other people in his or her life. The Adaptive Aggressive needs to take these other factors into account and then choose to bring out the higher side. If he or she does not make that choice, the higher side may not emerge on its own.

While Adaptive Aggressives often get ahead by using a relationship as a vehicle for their own growth, in and of itself that approach is not necessarily negative. Where it does become problematic is if they are on their low end, where a lack of balance can cause them to be ruthless. Then they may use other people to their own advantage, and they will continually look for the next opportunity. As soon as they identify a better situation or relationship than what they currently have, they may disengage and move on.

Indeed, the Adaptive Aggressive can be quite dangerous on the down side. They are aware of the world in which they live, and they tend to align themselves with questionable causes or even radical and harmful ones. Thus they may carry out deeds that serve their own interests but undermine everyone else's. At their lowest level they cannot be trusted for a second. They may betray others even as they are taking something from them.

Adaptive Aggressives on the low end include many of the M.B.A.s who enter banking, government, and industry with purely opportunistic goals in mind. They generally work for a Dynamic person, and they will be loyal to that Dynamic and do his or her work as long as they get promotions and have their backsides protected. If something they work on succeeds, Adaptive Aggressives will take credit for it. If it fails, they may avoid taking responsibility.

Many Adaptive Aggressives, though quite capable people, do not carry projects through to completion on their down side. They start all kinds of projects that just seem to evaporate. I often think of them as "emotional magicians" who create a lot of illusions in their lives. Like all good illusionists, they can be entertaining and exciting, but much of what they do amounts to distract-

187

ing motion. The potential of a project or idea excites them, but finishing it may require more emotional stability, determination, and focus than they have.

Adaptive Aggressives also have a difficult time expressing their emotions and revealing their true selves. Eventually their high level of self-criticism will be turned outward and applied to other people and to their environment. Indeed, they often try to change their environment because they find it dissatisfying. And if things do not go well, the Adaptive Aggressive, more than any other energy type, will cut and run. They will run out of a marriage, a relationship, or a job. Many Adaptive Aggressives repeat this pattern over and over again and fail to learn from the experience.

Open to the New—and to Now

But for every negative there's a positive, and that certainly holds true for this group. When they're in charge of their energy, one of the Adaptive Aggressives' positive qualities is that they are open to new ideas. If something excites them, they can go into the moment with openness and verve. They take advantage of the moment the way a football player sees an opening in the field and runs for a touchdown. On the up side, these openings in life will always appeal to the Adaptive Aggressive. And they will use their higher energies to plan for the future and determine how to get things done. They are smart and capable people who can calculate long-term plans. In this respect, then, their ability to scheme is a positive quality that allows them to formulate effective plans.

What's more, nobody is more attentive to details and to immediate follow-up than the Adaptive Aggressive; nobody organizes better. Without Adaptive Aggressives on a work team, the process of achieving an important goal can be chaotic, or even break down.

Adaptive Aggressives also have a great deal of flexibility and spontaneity, both of which compensate for any lack of creativity they may have. After all, what good are great ideas that sit around to gather dust and never get executed? The Adaptive Aggressive gets involved and makes sure things actually work. They're expert facilitators—and as such they serve a vital function.

When Adaptive Aggressives keep their energy high, they are not Machiavellis running around trying to take over the world or cheat their way to success. They are effective, can-do contributors to all the activities of life. They are exciting people to be with. They are flexible, in the moment, spontaneous, fluid, and fun. The other energies need that excitement. In truth, we are drawn to people who represent action, who do something worth reading about and considering. Witness the popularity of magazines and tabloids that continually show us people who have done something exciting.

WANT TO MAKE IT HAPPEN? HIRE AN ADAPTIVE AGGRESSIVE!

In the world of work, each of the life energy types has something essential to contribute. Typically the Dynamic Aggressives are the macromanagers, the ones who create and direct large organizational frameworks. Dynamic Assertives have input here, too, although they're less concerned with the directorial aspect of management, and more with the ideological. Once systems are outlined within these frameworks, Creative Assertives develop and refine the actual mechanics; then their plans are given to Adaptive Aggressives to see that they're implemented.

So it's the Adaptive Aggressives who actually make things happen. Masters of detail, they can set systems in motion, and if they're not always there for the long haul, the Adaptive Assertives—those organizational wizards who work just beneath them—are. Then, of course, there are the Adaptive Supportives, who contribute physically to the system with their hard work.

Concerning Adaptive Aggressives not sticking around for the long haul, this group tends to job-hop like crazy. They, like many others, make career choices based on what they believe will make them happy. But they rarely end up feeling happy or fulfilled with the work, and so they jump from one thing to another. Also, they tend to deny that they have failed at anything.

On the high end, Adaptive Aggressives do not like competition. Much like Creative Assertives in this respect, they don't think other people have the right to judge them. Adaptive Aggressives do not believe that their insights, skills, and creativity should be pitted against those of another, because they don't see themselves as being the same as anyone else. Also, they don't want to risk losing and being shown up. Therefore they generally don't want to play the game unless they write the rules.

Still, achievement is very important to the Adaptive

Aggressive. They believe that the more successful they are, the more other people will appreciate them. As a result they tend to exaggerate everything they do and will try to make themselves indispensable. This orientation toward achievement can make them quite effective in the workplace, especially when, on the high end, they follow through on details. Generally, though, Adaptive Aggressives are responsible only to the degree that they feel appreciated for their efforts. And they prefer to be responsible to a more powerful person. Then they really get the job done.

An Adaptive Aggressive is great at reading a crisis situation quickly and coming up with solutions. If someone presents a business problem to an Adaptive Aggressive, he or she will offer a dozen viable ways to resolve it. The other person will be drawn by these abilities. The catch: While on the up side, an Adaptive Aggressive helps another person with the intention of staying around for a while; on the down side, they help, but with the idea that doing so will get them to the next place they want to be.

Unfortunately, they do not always balance the ethical and moral implications of responsibility with the practical aspects. When they do value the moral implications of their actions, they can be conscientious, valuable contributors to an enterprise. But if they are operating from their lower energy, Adaptive Aggressives may start a lot of projects but rarely bring any to completion. They take shortcuts and look for instantaneous gratification, rather than execute a job from beginning to end. If something better comes along, they leave. Or they feel slighted, and leave.

Nevertheless, for facilitating short-term goals—no

matter how difficult—the Adaptive Aggressive is unparalleled. In fact, members of this group relish a challenge, and their willingness to confront difficulties head-on, rather than shrink from them, is one of their virtues. If something hard needs doing now, an Adaptive Aggressive is your best bet for getting it done.

A friend familiar with my views on the natural life energy groups emphasized this point in a conversation we had recently.

"Gary," she said, "I get the impression that you're not too crazy about Adaptive Aggressives because they can be exploitative. But there's another aspect to them—they are, in a sense, the most helpful group. They can be real life-savers, simply because they'll do things that no one else will do."

She went on to tell me about an experience she had years ago but that she still remembers vividly. It was her first day as a college freshman. The dorms were crowded that year. Settling into her room, she was disconcerted to find that although her two roommates had claimed desks, there was no third desk in the room for her. As a creative writer who liked to write on a hard surface, she felt that she was starting her higher education on a bad note.

But talking to the RA—the residential assistant who supposedly managed her hall—was no help. This person claimed that there was a furniture shortage and that no more student desks were available at the moment. All the RA had to offer was the prospect of filling out forms and waiting. The upstairs RA had the same story, and my friend suspected that although these people professed to care that she was starting her college career without a desk, her problem was not really a priority for them. She began to get discouraged about college even before her first class.

Yet the day was saved. What happened was that two girls who roomed next door got wind of the situation. These young women, whom my friend later got to know, were, she reports, classic Adaptive Aggressives. For instance, on that first day, although they hadn't been on campus much longer than she had, they had already scoped out the whole place, and they seemed to know a million people. They were loud, pushy, all-over-the-place types who would do anything.

And they proceeded to do just that.

First they immediately grasped the problem, and the fact that something had to be done before classes started. Then they told my friend that they'd seen where there was an unused desk. "Come on," they said to her, "let's go and get it. With three of us, we should be able to drag it to your room."

The desk was in an area that they were not authorized to go into. "Won't we get into trouble?" my friend asked. "This desk looks different from everyone else's. Besides, aren't I supposed to fill out a furniture request form and route it through the administration?"

These considerations meant nothing to the Adaptive Aggressive young women. "Don't be silly!" they said. "You need a desk, there's one here, and you're getting it!"

The problem was solved.

My friend reported that although she did later get to know the two helpful students next door, they never became friends. "I was a quiet Creative, they were obnoxious Adaptive Aggressives, and we didn't have much in common. But here's the important thing," she continued. "I needed something done. They, and nobody else, were the ones who could get the job done, and I'll always remember those two for that." She also says that thinking about that incident helps her see how people of each life energy type, no matter how alien or annoying that energy might seem to different types, can work to support the well-being of others.

And on their up side, Adaptive Aggressives *are* supportive. They can do a great job as part of a work team that includes creative people, since they have the capacity to follow through on a good idea and handle all the details. They can also take someone's work and present it to the public. The Adaptive Aggressive generally likes the limelight and enjoys interfacing with others, while the Creative may prefer to work behind the scenes.

The Conditioned Aggressive

By the way, there is an interesting "dual energy" phenomenon that we see with some people who are Adaptive Aggressives and Dynamic Aggressives in the workplace. These people, while aggressive and authoritative at work, are passive and obedient at home. They seem to have succeeded at mastering two energies. But the natural energy is always the one that does not make a person feel conflicted. In some cases the dominant role these Aggressives play at work will be their real energy. They remain passive at home, even though they hate the role, because they were conditioned to be Adaptive Supportives.

More often, however, the role a person plays at home represents his or her real energy. We tend to reveal our true selves in personal relationships because it is in these that we are most vulnerable. Generally, then, people who are Adaptive Supportives at home truly are that way. They present their conditioned, Aggressive self at work to achieve certain goals, even if they must be insensitive to others. If they were to be submissive at work, they would not get raises and promotions. If they did not get raises and promotions, their partner at home (who may be a true Dynamic!) would not be satisfied with the relationship. Thus a person will play out his or her conditioned self to sustain the relationship of the true self.

EXCITING—OR EXPLOITATIVE— RELATIONSHIPS

Relationships are important to Adaptive Aggressives, on the down side because they use relationships as tools. This is the energy group whose favored means of coping is to distract themselves with visions of future glory, and other people become the means for achieving goals related to these visions. So where others might derive spiritual nourishment from relationships, Adaptive Aggressives nourish themselves with the fads and addictions offered by society, using relationships as means to this end.

Their specialty is attaching themselves to powerful people. And they're good at this because they can be appealingly exciting. They are adventurous, energetic, and able to take on the energy of another person at any time. This unique ability can lead other people to believe that an Adaptive Aggressive is the perfect person for them. This is especially the case with powerful or influential people who, because of their lifestyles, are often short on friends. Along comes someone who seems like the answer to a prayer. What they like, the Adaptive Aggressive likes. The apparent similarities are enticing. The other person may think, "God, this is really a great person. We're so much alike." Perhaps. But the similarities may be an illusion. And the Adaptive Aggressive may in fact be manipulating the relationship because he or she has an ulterior motive.

Whether you're a power broker or not, a relationship with an Adaptive Aggressive can be a complicated and tricky thing because they bring a lot of expectations and emotional baggage into it. But they won't show you that at the outset. So it's as if, initially, they come into your life with a little suitcase of emotions. And then once they feel that they've got you, the doorbell rings, you go to the door, and there are twenty-seven tractor-trailer-loads of emotions they want to bring in!

Many Adaptive Aggressives do not have close friendships. They are afraid to trust people or let people really get to know them. Thus they can be quite lonely. Compounding their interpersonal problems is their inability to take criticism well. It makes them feel too unworthy, and it often mirrors what they've been telling themselves all along. In general they anticipate negativity from others and don't want to risk being brought down from good feelings.

Members of this energy group can have a "here today, gone tomorrow" air that makes other people not even bother to keep their telephone number. They always seem to be halfway out the door, and this lack of stability is another factor preventing Adaptive Aggressives from forming strong friendships. They are too unpredictable and skittish to establish a sense of permanence. But all their activity is something of a cover-up for identity problems.

These same identity problems can trouble an Adaptive Aggressive's relationship with his or her children. They tend to pressure their children to achieve what they have not. The child becomes an extension of the parent's ego, which is not a healthy situation for either of them.

Actually, problems begin in many Adaptive Aggressive-run families before the achievement stage, with infancy. Adaptive Aggressive parents bore easily, so they don't have the inner resources to change their usual mental rhythms to relate to a baby for any length of time. They're the type who say, "I can't get into this diaper-changing stage, but once the kid starts to talk, it'll be interesting, so I'll get involved." Then, when the child starts to talk, it's interesting, all right—for about five minutes. The Adaptive Aggressive does not have a long attention span or much patience, and the toddler stage, like all other phases of childhood, requires a great deal of patience. In addition, Adaptive Aggressives may be too preoccupied with their own professional interests to give their children much time. They *are* good at providing their children with material things; in fact, they're highly responsible in this regard. But they may not be able to meet children's needs for large blocks of parental time and for unconditional love.

Have We Got an Adaptive Aggressive for You!

A more positive facet of Adaptive Aggressives in relationships is that they're great partners for just plain having fun with. They're spontaneous, they like adventure, and they're full of raw energy. Not everyone appreciates these attributes. But for those who do, an Adaptive Aggressive on his or her high side can be a perfect partner.

Who can best pair with an Adaptive Aggressive? A Dynamic Aggressive or a Dynamic Assertive. They're the ones most likely to have the energy level, smarts, and backbone necessary to tangle with this type. And these Dynamics are attracted by Adaptive Aggressives because they're usually looking for someone who agrees with them, who compliments them, who's willing to do what they like to do, and, if work is part of the equation, who can help implement their ideas and plans. Adaptive Aggressives fit the bill in these ways. What's more, while most people are intimidated by the two fast-moving Dynamic energies, Adaptive Aggressives are not. That's a big plus from the point of view of the Dynamic who is tired of being shied away from. Dynamic Aggressives and Assertives can be volatile, demanding, and even insulting to their intimates and work partners, but Adaptive Aggressives can take whatever's dished out. They're tough. And so if they can keep their exploitative tendencies in check, they can make good matches for the two most demanding Dynamic types.

If collaborative work is part of the relationship picture, Adaptive Aggressives can serve as effective lieutenants for these Dynamics. On their high side they'll remain loyal to their Dynamic counterparts through adversity. Of course, their low-side potential for disloyalty and betrayal is always a danger. Consider Elvis Presley, a classic Dynamic Assertive who often surrounded himself with Adaptive Aggressives. Like many Dynamic Assertives, Elvis wanted people around who would understand him, agree with him, and be willing to do what he liked to do. But he ended up being exploited to the hilt. His "friends" betrayed his confidence by writing books that revealed every little thing they knew about him.

While the Dynamic Aggressive and Assertive may sometimes be up to the challenge of a relationship with an Adaptive Aggressive, a Dynamic Supportive has a harder time of it. Consider an Adaptive Aggressive woman who marries a Dynamic Supportive man. She may think she can motivate her more mellow husband to help her achieve certain material ambitions. But when this unrealistic scenario doesn't work out, it's all downhill after that.

Interestingly, the Dynamic Supportive man may not realize this until the bitter end. The Adaptive Aggressive is the type who will leave her mate and only then tell him all the things he "did wrong" over the years, or all the things she couldn't stand about him. She never brought these things up at the time, because then there was still some benefit that could be squeezed out of the person. But the whole story finally comes out in the end, which is one of the reasons that breaking up with an Adaptive Aggressive is hard to do. The other one is that they will generally seek a large settlement for their trouble. And even if you're talking about a parting of the ways of friends and not about a romantic relationship breakup, this can be the case. Sometimes it seems as if you practically need a written pre-friendship agreement before you get involved with an Adaptive Aggressive!

SPIRITUALITY NOT A PRIORITY

Spiritual growth is not a priority for Adaptive Aggressives. Instead, they seek intellectual growth to acquire new skills, and perhaps emotional growth to help them better adapt. They are also interested in physical development, and will often take pride in their bodies.

Adaptive Aggressives have a lot of peak experiences because they are more willing than other energy types to try new things. One of the reasons they are exciting people on the up side is that they will do things that other people would never even consider. They welcome new experiences, which, in a world peopled mostly by frightened, let's-stick-to-what-we-know types, is like a breath of fresh air. On the down side, however, they may have peak experiences that are not necessarily constructive for themselves and others.

Sometimes Adaptive Aggressives take a stab at spiritual enlightenment, but they do so more in form than in essence. For instance, they may treat spiritual events as yet another opportunity to maneuver themselves into someone else's life. Go to any New Age retreat, for example, and many of the people there will be Adaptive Aggressives. But they never surrender to the experience because they need to be in control at all times. They're the ones who meditate with their eyes open, the ones who are supposed to be in a deep sleep but are thinking all the while. To grow, you have to let go, and they generally can't.

The Adaptive Aggressive may be involved in personal improvement, but the effort is likely to fit into their utilitarian scheme of things in some way. Reading is not an idle intellectual adventure for them; it's a get-ahead thing. An Adaptive Aggressive might be the type of person who litters the coffee table with art books, philosophy books, and *New Yorker* magazines, while hidden underneath they have copies of *People*. Their true interest lies with techniques for getting ahead, making deals, dressing for success, picking up men, picking up women, etc. They're always looking for an advantage and a way to better their circumstances.

CAN YOU MOVE TOWARD TRUST?

If you're an Adaptive Aggressive, it doesn't mean you are doomed to be a chronic user, or a loner. You can have a balanced work life and mutually fulfilling relationships if you try. But there are a couple of issues you'll have to work through first.

To begin with, you have a particular energy—one that's very strong—and you should honor it. But you can refine and channel it to get along more harmoniously in the world. You can learn to harness your power and control your energy, in order to construct positive relationships and achievements. Your energy should be constant, like the electricity that supplies a light bulb. If it's like the electricity that causes lightning, it will be spectacular and exciting, but also spastic, undependable, and potentially harmful.

Think about your life. Do you continually start and stop projects due to the spastic quality of your energy? Do you feel powerless and trapped when you find yourself in relationships that require commitment and stability? Do you feel angry when you can no longer control everything around you? If so, begin to recognize that these are excuses not to relate to others. They are problems you need to work on.

Your energy must be harnessed and developed to its highest level so it can be applied in a positive way. Learn to accept being alone as a constructive state, rather than dwelling on the negative feelings that come from loneliness. Move away from being manipulative and predatory, and you will be freer to exhibit your sharing and caring qualities.

Learn to identify environments that will suit your energy. You have as much potential as any other energy type—perhaps more—to be happy with your energy. But you may be so caught up in searching for something that you fail to look at what you already have. Or you may come across a healthy environment for yourself but pass it right by in your haste. Look for situations that satisfy the needs of your energy type—ideally, you need to be acknowledged for your special skills and attributes, to cooperate rather than compete with other people, and to avoid the harsh judgment of others.

Adaptive Aggressives tend to look outward. That's okay up to a point; we all need feedback to see how we're functioning. But if a person is to grow, he or she must begin to turn inward. So stop looking to others all the time to validate and improve your life. You may be in a terrible bind because you don't trust others, yet you depend on other people for so much. As a result you may feel resentful when you don't find satisfaction in the things other people bring to your life.

Concentrate on appreciating yourself. Learn to be less harsh on yourself and to trust your own competence. You must learn to love someone affectionately rather than for the qualities that serve your needs or allow you to live vicariously. The extreme swings in your feelings, from idealizing others to being overly negative, can drive other people away. Like many Adaptive Aggressives, you will get fed up with the things you do to ingratiate yourself to others, and end up feeling enraged.

Adaptive Aggressives, in particular, have the potential to grow and become more genuine if they form relationships with people who treat them with kindness and regard. But you must overcome some difficult obstacles to establish such relationships. Most important, ask yourself, "Can I work on becoming more trusting, and more able to experience others as benign and caring?"

If the answer is no, you may continue to manipulate and mistreat people, and they will not tolerate such treatment for long.

But if you've answered yes, you'll have taken the first step toward making the most of your exciting, powerful, and potentially fulfilling life energy.

CONCLUSION

What We Can Learn
From One Another

After reading about the seven natural life energy types you probably have some idea about which type best describes you. To test your idea and review the concepts in the foregoing chapters, you can take the quizzes at the end of this book. They will help you determine which type you are, although keep in mind that people's life energy identities are not always clear-cut; you may display attributes from two or three predominant types. But whatever the case, you might at this point be asking the following question: If I am a particular NLE type (or types), does that mean that I must necessarily, and always, display a particular pattern of behavior?

The answer is, of course, no. As a member of a particular energy group, you may *tend* to display a certain pattern, but that's not at all the same as saying that you're destined to act in a certain way. We are, after all, unique individuals and possessors of free will.

It is with this idea of the personal freedom that we each possess that I conclude this book with the following thought: Each natural life energy has something of value about it that members of any other energy group can emulate. This is not to say that, for instance, an Adaptive Supportive can or should decide to turn himself into a Dynamic Aggressive. But it is to say that there is at least one characteristically Dynamic Aggressive trait that an Adaptive Supportive, or anyone else, might try now and then to incorporate into his or her life.

So let's start here, with Dynamic Aggressives. What is there about the Dynamic Aggressive energy that might serve as a model for anyone? We know that this group's defining quality is that they exhibit a tremendous drive to get to the top, and, in truth, we don't want the rest of the world emulating this; it would be too much of an unnatural strain for most people, not to mention the fact that it would result in unparalleled bloodshed. But there *is* something about Dynamic Aggressives that people of all energy types could emulate: their affinity for hard work. A member of any energy group could benefit from injecting a little more of the work ethic into his or her life—at particular times, anyway. So when these times come up, a Dynamic Aggressive could be an appropriate inspiration for anyone.

Likewise, not everyone could or should go around spouting opinions on how to change the world, as is the wont of Dynamic Assertives. But there is something about Dynamic Assertives that others might want to observe and learn from. Specifically, Dynamic Assertives depend on multiple, as opposed to single, interpersonal relationships. They are the ones who best understand that no one individual can fill all a person's relationship needs, and even that relationships themselves cannot fill all our emotional and intellectual needs. That's why Dynamic Assertives tend to have a variety of people coming into and going out of their lives, and sometimes to have low-intimacy withdrawal periods.

The way Dynamic Assertives live in this regard is somewhat unconventional, and no one is saying that everyone should follow suit. But by at least observing and thinking about the Dynamic Assertives' way, perhaps those individuals of other energy types who are too clingy and relationship-dependent can change their perspective into a more realistic one.

What does the Dynamic Supportive have to show us? Most of us are not, after all, constitutionally cut out to become nurturing helpers in the Dynamic Supportive mode. But we can all try to emulate the group's warmth and friendliness. Sure, if we all tried this, our imitative efforts would be a superficial thing (and maybe the whole world would begin to seem like Southern California!). Still, communicating in a more pleasant way might be beneficial anyway.

We can't all be Picassos or Shakespeares, and there's no use trying, but there is a trait of Creative Assertives that anyone can try to develop. Creatives have associative minds. It's the way they create—they look at a thing and, instead of connecting that thing with what it's usually associated with, they let their mind wander all over the place to create new associations. And any person can do mental exercises to develop a loose, wandering, associative mind, like the Creative's. This may be difficult at first, but it's doable by anyone and probably helpful for everyone in that it would increase people's problem-solving skills.

What can we learn from Adaptive Supportives? Probably not how to become millionaires; this is not their forte. Nor is innovative thinking. But a hallmark of this group is devotion to family values—meant in all the positive ways. This is the group that stresses family in their social lives and in their loyalties, and in today's rootless, transient society, standing by one's kin is a virtue that should be encouraged whenever possible.

As for Adaptive Assertives, one of the things this conscientious group can demonstrate for us is the virtue of being well organized. Whatever energy you have and whatever work you do, being neat and organized will help you optimize your life.

Turning to our last energy group, while some Adaptive Aggressives might be able to offer us seminars on how to back-stab your way to the top, this is not the area in which we should emulate them. But we could all look to their openness to opportunity.

It's sad, but some of us don't even concede the existence of opportunity. And while others may wait for opportunity to knock, the Adaptive Aggressive is the one who's got the door wide open and is ready to sprint out and meet opportunity halfway down the block! This is a great spirit to have. After all, how many times do you hear excuses as people fail to grasp good things that come their way?

"Oh, I don't have the energy for that."

"Oh, that would be too much trouble."

"It would never work out."

"They won't like me."

"I couldn't."

These are defeatist attitudes that you don't find Adaptive Aggressives hobbling themselves with. We could all learn from them in that.

Finally, whatever your NLE type, and whatever you choose to learn from those living out different energies, one thing is certain. If you are living out your own on the high side, with respect for your own unique gifts, you will be teaching others even as you learn from them.

APPENDIX:
TEST YOURSELF—
WHICH TYPE ARE YOU?

The following series of quizzes is intended to help you determine your predominant natural life energy type, or types. Go to any sections you think might apply to you—there may be as many as three or four—and answer the *true-false* questions in them. Be honest; answer *true* only if a statement seems highly applicable to you. If a statement represents only something you *wish* were true, or something you think others would like to see in you, answer *false*.

In general, answering *true* to six or more out of the eight questions in a quiz means that you are that type. But since every individual is unique and has a different constellation of attributes and attitudes, you may not fit into any NLE pattern that definitively. Therefore, look to whichever quiz yields the highest number of *trues*. This is your predominant energy.

Am I a Dynamic Aggressive?

1. Ever since childhood, I've always seemed to want more out of life than my peers did.
2. I can work harder than most people, and I enjoy doing so.
3. I spend much less time than others do on what I consider pointless leisure pursuits, such as TV- and movie-watching; novel-reading; and card-, computer-, or board-game playing.
4. I find myself getting frustrated because most people operate at a slower pace than I do.
5. I could never be really happy working for someone else.
6. I don't have much time or patience for long family gatherings, such as a whole afternoon spent celebrating Thanksgiving.
7. Managing a big job and having underlings carry out the detail work is my ideal kind of endeavor.
8. I'm more intelligent than most people, and others almost always recognize this.

Am I a Dynamic Assertive?

1. I enjoy thinking about large issues, such as how society is organized politically.
2. The idea of a lifelong and exclusive intimate partner doesn't seem desirable or realistic for me.
3. Being alone does not scare me; in fact, I do some of my best thinking when I'm alone.
4. I find myself getting frustrated because most people's worldview is so limited.
5. I have a drive to express my ideas and influence the thinking of others.
6. I have no trouble getting people to listen to me and grasp what I'm saying.
7. The make-up of my social circle is constantly changing.
8. I can't fathom the idea of holding one job for decades.

Am I a Dynamic Supportive?

1. I get asked for help a lot, and have a hard time saying no.
2. When I meet a person I'll give that individual the benefit of the doubt; in other words, I'll like him until he gives me a reason not to.
3. I procrastinate a lot.
4. People usually like me.
5. I'm happiest interacting with people and aiding them in some way.
6. It sometimes takes an outside force to get me motivated because I tend to be satisfied with what I have.
7. People tell me I have a great sense of humor.
8. I'm good at smoothing over others' conflicts and helping to mediate them.

Am I a Creative Assertive?

1. When I'm in a new situation, such as a new job setting or relationship, I spend a lot of time comparing it to analogous situations I've been in previously.
2. I can sometimes work creatively at full throttle for hours on end and not notice the passage of time.
3. I'll periodically go through extremely low-energy periods during which I have to remind myself that it's only a phase.
4. I find myself getting frustrated because most people are not on my mental wavelength.
5. Working by myself is no problem; in fact, I prefer it.
6. At times, ideas just "come to me," and if I can't put them down then and there—on paper, canvas, etc.—I'll be uncomfortable until I can.
7. Throughout my life there's been a pattern of people calling me one or more of the following: "temperamental," "moody," "sad," "flighty," "different"; and I never really felt like I was "one of the boys," or girls.
8. I find competition distasteful.

Am I an Adaptive Supportive?

1. I believe that respect for authority is one of the cornerstones of good character.
2. A lifelong relationship with a romantic partner is one of my goals.
3. My extended family is the most important part of my social life.
4. Directing a big job and supervising a lot of underlings is my idea of a headache.
5. Holding one job for decades would be okay with me if the conditions were good and the boss was nice.
6. Trying to lengthen your life by eating the "right" foods doesn't make much sense to me because when your time's up, your time's up.
7. I believe that blood is thicker than water and that it's more important to be loyal to your relatives than to your friends.
8. I prefer to work at a job a set number of hours each day and then have the rest of the twenty-four hours for relaxation.

Am I an Adaptive Assertive?

1. I feel I'm good at supervising a small group of people, and I enjoy doing so.
2. I believe that divorce is to be strongly avoided whenever possible.
3. When it comes to spending and savings habits, I take pride in being more thrifty and less foolish than most people.
4. I generally believe that if individuals behave outside the norms of society, they should be prepared to pay the price.
5. My home is more organized and cleaner than most people's in my neighborhood.
6. I enjoy the feeling of my life going along at an even pace like a well-oiled machine; too many stops and starts and ups and downs would really upset me.
7. I understand that detail work is what ultimately gets a job done, and I have the gumption and know-how to tackle details.
8. I would never dress in a flashy, bohemian, or otherwise attention-getting way.

Am I an Adaptive Aggressive?

1. When I first enter a new environment, such as a workplace or a school, I make it a point to become acquainted with as many people as possible.
2. I rarely seek quiet.
3. My vacations are always highly structured; several days of just sitting in one place and vegetating would drive me crazy.
4. Networking as a career and life tool is something that comes naturally to me.
5. When tackling a problem or task, I'm usually less defeatist than others.
6. I like associating with influential people and am not intimidated by them.
7. I'm happiest moving and doing, as opposed to sitting and thinking.
8. I thrive on setting goals for myself and then figuring out how to reach them; I can't imagine just drifting through life without a plan.